Stronger Than I Thought

A Bridge of Hope Through Heartbreak and Pain
Find Your Breakthrough and Soar

Nancy Ormon

ISBN: 979-8-9852068-0-7 Paperback
      979-8-9852068-1-4 eBook

FREE BONUS WORKBOOK

THANK YOU SO MUCH FOR CHOOSING TO READ MY BOOK.

I pray it is a blessing to you and those you share it with. To enhance your Quiet Time and Times of Reflection, request your download of the companion workbook at:

https://nancyormon.com

Dedication

Blake spraying sunflowers 2003

This book is dedicated to...

My Son, Blake

Even though Your life here on this earth was short,
you left a legacy that lives on today.
The lives you touched are those who will never
forget how you made a difference.
I miss your hugs. I miss your smile, I miss your
loving heart.

Love you, Mom

Contents

Introduction

In late June of 2010, Darrel Ferguson, a well-known Elder to the Pentecostal Church of South Africa, visited our church and sat beside me. During worship, he leaned over and whispered to me, "God says: I will." I thanked him for sharing this information with me and prayed under my breath for God to show me whether he had *truly* spoken to this man and if He had, what 'I will' meant.

A few days later, I went to lunch with a friend. We ran into this same man, who was having lunch with another pastor and their wives. I stopped by and thanked him again for the information he had given me and told him I was still praying about it. He pulled up a chair for me and ask me to sit for a few minutes. He began to talk with me about how many times God says, 'I will' in the Bible and then he started asking me questions. He asked me if I had a lot of notes written down about my experiences with God, and I told him I did. He told me I need to start writing and that, when I did, God would help my writing flow.

I went home that afternoon and wrote down everything he had told me. My journal from that day reads, "I am committing to writing down all my experiences with God." I did not start my book until April 10, 2014, after I read in my Bible, "Thus speaks the Lord God of Israel, saying: Write in a book for yourself all the words that I have spoken to you. **Jeremiah 30:2**" I circled the verse in my Bible and wrote it in my journal. On May 7, 2014, I started my book, but I soon received discouragement from someone I had asked to review it and I stopped writing after two chapters.

On August 14th, 2014, I was in Oklahoma teaching at a women's conference and attending a workshop with an incredible pastor I had never met before. She spoke to me and said that my reward would be on paper. She said that my writing was all about obedience and then she told my friend that she saw an arm and paper. The lines on the paper were blank, though, because I hadn't been writing. Now, seven years later, I am isolated at home with health challenges and I'm ready to write. Now is the time for me to be obedient.

———————————

As I begin to share my story, I have a few questions for you.

- Have you have ever had a broken heart?
- Have you ever had fears of the unknown? Maybe in your health or marriage or emotional health?

- Have you ever felt so tired you didn't think you could take even one more step because what you were going through was just too hard?
- Have you ever been confused to the point that it stops you in your tracks?

My story is a story of healing. I was diagnosed with Multiple Sclerosis in 1984 and had so many fears of the unknown. God manifested my healing on July 18, 2001, because I *believed* His word and took it for my own. God healed my broken heart after my first-born son died in a plane crash at the age of 26. I learned about God's faithfulness. I learned I could get through any adversity with His help. In 2020, I had acute renal failure. Kidneys shut down, suddenly, with no health problems. I was fine one day, and not the next. I learned endurance and keeping my focus on him, as I waited 10 months for a donor and transplant.

I want to present the lessons that I've learned here about:
- Grace
- Unanswered prayers
- Our Biblical identity in Christ
- Peace
- Hearing God's voice and discerning His plans for our lives.

Since learning these lessons on my own, I have been a speaker at women conferences. I have ministered as a Volunteer Chaplain at a hospital. I have led Bible studies. I have spoken at several funerals and celebrations of life, and there has never been a moment when God's presence was not with me.

I have also seen other people make decisions for Christ because their hearts were open, and because they were desperate for a better way of life. Many of these people came out of experiences of adversity with a renewal of strength, hope, and direction, as well as a passion to serve other people.

Over the next few pages, I want to teach you how to grow through endurance by putting your trust in what you know and not what you don't know. I am confident that you can gain more knowledge of God's plan for your life by internalizing these lessons and looking to Him for redemption during adversity. I am also confident that, if you share these stories with other people, you can give them hope for their future.

Chapter 1
Hearing God's Voice

Recently, I was asked to be on a podcast to share my story, and I talked many times about how God speaks to me. When my granddaughter, Harper, listened to the podcast, she was full of questions about how this worked.

"Nana," she asked, "how old were you when God started talking to you?"

I thought back and told her, "I would say I was in my late 30s when I started recognizing His voice."

When I was in my thirties, I was attending a conference called A Walk to Emmaus. I really didn't want to be there because I was still grieving. Just before I attended the conference, my 15-year-old niece, Nancy Roxanne Wilhite, had been killed in a car accident and I couldn't understand the loss. Sitting alone in a swing in the sweltering heat, though, I opened my heart to God by asking, "Why am I here? What do you want me to learn?"

Over the next several days, God made it clear to me that He had Nancy. Her time on this earth was finished, but she was in a good place. Life is very hard, and I might never understand it, but when I opened my heart to God, He gave me a peace that passed all understanding (**Phil. 4:7**).

At one of the evening events, I felt so loved by God that it changed my life forever. I felt a love that I had not experienced before, and I finally understood that God wanted a relationship with me. Not just a Sunday morning relationship either. He wanted me to know His love and to know His love *daily*. This was eye opening for me and I went back home a changed person. Before that conference, I cursed a lot. I didn't watch my words. My heart was self-centered. After that conference, I wanted to change everything in my life and that was when I started to hear God's voice.

In her Study Bible, Joyce Meyer writes that, "God wants us to listen to Him, so he speaks to us through a voice we will recognize. Sometimes it may sound like our own voice; sometimes it may sound like the voice of someone we know. BUT the point is that the voice will always bring people peace when God speaks to us." In **1 Samuel 3:4-7**, the Lord calls Samuel to Him, but Samuel runs to his father, Eli, saying, "Here I am." When the Lord calls Samuel a second and third time, Eli runs to him again. Verse 7 reads, "Now Samuel did not yet know the Lord, and the word of the Lord was not yet revealed to him," A few moments later, Eli helps Samuel to understand that the voice He is hearing is God's voice. God spoke to Samuel in a voice that was familiar to him so he wouldn't be afraid.

I can vouch for these experiences with the stories I will share in this book. Sometimes people think God's voice is going to be like a big, scary sonic boom. Other people think that hearing from God is a supernatural manifestation, but I've never experienced God in this way. Most of the time, God speaks in our hearts through peace or a lack of it. He speaks through wisdom and common sense. He doesn't lead us to do foolish things. In my own life, God has spoken to me through other people, through journaling, through His word, and through prayer. He has never spoken to me audibly during this time, but I feel him in my spirit. In times of joy and in times of defeat, His voice gives me comfort and peace. When I seek Him, I find Him (**Jeremiah 29:13**). If you seek Him, you will find Him and He will speak to you clearly.

A Life Changing Moment

After listening to my story, my little Harper was suddenly curious. I asked her if she wanted to hear from God and she told me that she did. I told her to pray to God and ask him to open her heart so she could hear Him speak to her. The next day she Facetimed me with a precious story. She was quietly excited. She was looking for something in her room and came across a little toy fortune cookie that she'd left in her drawer, forgotten. She opened it to recall what was inside and found a little piece of paper with a message typed on it and a little bracelet with a feather on it. The message on the paper read, "Don't be afraid to spread your wings."

To Harper, this message reminded her of her Uncle Blake who was killed in a plane crash. We had always talked about feathers and how Blake got his wings like the angels in heaven. She asked me then, "How do I know if I am just making this up or if God really spoke to me?" I asked her, "Did you pray for Him to speak to you?" She had. Then I told her that when she asked God for answers or help, she would know when He answered her because she would experience peace. From there, her interest in God's word has begun to grow and she is now growing in her faith with a daily reading of scripture.

Three Mental Barriers

In my own daily reading of scripture, I have been following a series of lessons by Mark Batterson. Batterson talks about the Three Mental Barriers to hearing God's voice, writing, "We've all noticed that the quality of reception on a cell phone varies widely. The same is true with us. We must be positioned correctly to hear God speak. Sometimes we never give God a chance to talk to us. We've made up our minds.

We want to do what we want to do; not what God wants us to do. Our hearts are hardened, and we're unwilling to listen. But if you really want to hear from God" he continues, "you have to understand what is keeping you from hearing God. There are three mental barriers that keep your mind closed to God's message.

1. **Pride.** If you think you don't need God in your life and want to handle things yourself, you're probably not listening for God to speak. Pride keeps you from being open to the possibility that God might want to say something to you.
2. **Fear.** A lot of people can't hear God speak because they're afraid to hear God speak. Maybe you think that hearing God's voice makes you a religious fanatic.
3. **Bitterness.** When you hold on to hurt, resentment, or a grudge, then you're not going to be able to hear God, because your heart is hardened. It has grown cold and made you defensive, even to God's love."

To continue, Batterson states, "Some of you have been hurt badly, whether it happened this week or years ago, and you're still holding on to it. I want to tell you that you've got to let it go. Not for their sake, but for your sake. That resentment is killing you! It is a self-inflicted wound that allows people from your past to continue to hurt you today. You need to let it go, not because they deserve forgiveness but because you need to get on with your life."

These are strong words of wisdom. As I reflect on these words, I remember sitting in that swing in the sweltering heat and opening my heart to God. A sense of pride and bitterness were feelings I was experiencing. Pride, thinking I did not need to be here, and bitterness over my niece's death.

As you continue reading this book, you will see how—when I released some of my bitterness to God—He started to speak to me through so many circumstances. You will see how He has spoken to me through other people, through whispers, through peacefulness, through His word. If hearing God's voice is something you want, I encourage you to stop reading now and to ask God to speak to you. Ask Him to open your heart and your eyes and show you who He is, with peace and understanding.

REFLECTION POINTS

- Hearing God's voice is a key to strengthening your walk with God
- There are three mental barriers that can prevent you from hearing God's voice: Pride, Fear, and Bitterness

Chapter 2
Diagnosis of Multiple Sclerosis

Before we get too far along, I want to share a bit about myself. I grew up in a very small farm town in the west Texas Panhandle with a family of six kids. There were five girls and one boy; my parents couldn't give up on kids until they got that boy and, as the youngest, my sisters and I thought he was spoiled. From the oldest to the youngest, we were spread out over 13 years. I was number 4—right in the middle of the bunch—but we now have 79 immediate family members, including kids, grandkids, great grandkids and great-great grandkids! We have always been a close family and carry on that legacy today.

My parents were hard-working and they provided us what we needed. My dad owned his own business, and my mom worked part-time while taking care of all six kids. We learned to appreciate hard work at an early age; we all had chores and we all shared the responsibility of cooking dinner after school while my mom was working. If we wanted to be cheerleaders or to play in the band, we had to work to earn the money to pay the expenses ourselves. My brother was an avid runner, so he didn't have near the expenses all us girls had.

My parents took us to church and sometimes they attended with us. At 12 years of age, I asked Jesus into my heart. My parents always made sure that we had opportunities to attend church activities, and I am thankful for that. We learned the importance of going to church, but beyond attendance, my parents did not talk about God until later in life. They are both in heaven now, along with one of my sisters, Beth.

I was married right out of high school to my childhood sweetheart. We had two precious little boys and lived on a farm. I loved the farm life. I loved driving the tractor and helping with harvest. It was hard work. Farming is a career that will test your faith because you are at the mercy of weather and the economy. At the time, I did not have a close relationship with God. I based my happiness on 'things.' I was not happy with our marriage either so, after seven years, with nothing in common but our boys, I wanted out. I was 25 years old.

After a year and a half, I met my husband, Tommy, and we married three months later. It happened very fast. We had a daughter, Chelsea Lake. Now, it was me, Tommy, Chelsea, Blake, and Scott. Tommy and I have gone through a lot of ups and downs in our marriage. All marriages have ups and downs though, and God has extended a lot of grace and mercy to both of us over the past 39 years. While we have experienced a lot of pain, we have also experienced a lot of joy and I would not change anything. That is why we are where we are today. We have both grown tremendously in our walk with God and we have grown together.

Never Knew

In 1984, two years into my marriage to Tommy, I was diagnosed with Multiple Sclerosis. It is an auto-immune disease that can be chronic progressive or relapsing remitting. One morning, I got up to run and found that my right leg was numb and tingling. Over the next week, I lost feeling in my lower body, from the waist down. After numerous tests, the diagnosis was clear. I had Multiple Sclerosis. I was relieved to learn that I had the relapsing/remitting type of MS, which was the best-case scenario. Most people would not know that I had the disease unless I told them. Once a week, I took shots to prevent the progression of the disease.

I still had numbness and tingling all the time and I could not run anymore. When I went out for daily walks, the tingling was so bad, that I often had to stop. I started speaking a positive affirmation as I would walk, saying, "It's not what the MS can do to me, it's what I can do to the MS." Over time, I'd repeat this to myself in sync with my walking.

Two months after my diagnosis, my sister, Beth, began to experience the same symptoms I had and she was also diagnosed with Multiple Sclerosis. Per studies I have read, Multiple Sclerosis is not a genetic disease. Beth's MS started out aggressive, and it took six months for her treatment team to really get a handle on what was wrong with her. I hated that her illness progressed so quickly. In only a few years, she was in a wheelchair.

I did not ask God to heal me, because, compared to my sister, my life hadn't really changed very much. I just had to take shots and a lot of precautions. I would have felt selfish asking God for help. At that point, I did not understand all the healing spoken about in God's word, because I was still only *playing church*; I went to church on Sunday, but I lived my life exactly how I wanted to live it. I just went on living with MS and dealing with symptoms and setbacks as they occurred.

My Healing, My Belief

In July of 2001, I was in a much better place with the Lord. One afternoon my friend, Jaynette, who lived a few houses down the street from me, called me up to talk to me about an up and coming move to Dallas our family was making. Jaynette and I always had great conversations about God, and she was a bright light everywhere she went. She was also a great influence in my life at the time. Over the phone, she told me that she wanted to pray for me because she felt that the Holy Spirit was leading her to ask for my healing from Multiple Sclerosis. It was not planned. It just happened. Her prayer was simple, but it hit my heart. There were no lightning bolts, no bells, no whistles. Everything was exactly the same, but in another way, *nothing* was the same because I now believed that I was healed.

In **Ephesians 3:20-21**, God tells us, "Now to Him who able to do immeasurably more than all we ask or imagine, according to his power that is at work within us, to him be glory in the church and in Christ Jesus throughout all generations, for ever and ever! Amen." Ephesians teaches us that God can do exceedingly and abundantly above and beyond all that we dare to hope, ask, or think. It is His power and it is done through us. He wants us to be daring in our faith and in our prayers. In my conversation with Jaynette, I felt God stretching my faith. My numbness did not go away—I still had tingling—but I was healed. Daily, I thanked Him for my healing.

It's Not Over

I accepted and believed in my healing on July 18, 2001, and I did not go back to the doctor. I stopped my shots and, when I went to doctor's appointments for other illnesses, I explained on the paperwork that I had previously had MS. I often used this as an opportunity to tell these doctors that I was healed and, though they shrugged that off, I stood strong in my belief.

Seventeen years later, in July of 2018, I had to return to the doctor once again. I'd started having new MS symptoms—numbness, tingling—and I felt very confused. I simply could not believe that God would manifest my healing, only to let the enemy come back and lay it on me again.

When this last episode of new symptoms came about, I called my previous pastor, Norman Chimunda, in Dallas and told him what was going on. He reminded me of several Bible stories where the enemy came back to God's people to attack again. In **2 Samuel 5:17-25**, for example, King David defeats the Philistines only to have to fight them again soon after. 2 Samuel teaches us that the enemy you overcome today may come back again and fight you tomorrow, but through faith in God, you can overcome the enemy again and again no matter which way or direction that it comes from.

Mark 5:21-43 offers similar lessons about healing and faith. We learn that things may get worse after prayer before they become better! Jairus' daughter was sick when he talked to Jesus, but she died before Jesus got to his home. Someone asks, "Your daughter is dead, why do you bother the master any further?" and this commentary from an outsider reminds us that Satan will try to discourage you on the way to your miracle and victory by telling you more bad news. The idea is for you to abandon your original desire from God and to accept the situation. Jesus's response to the bad news is: Do not fear, or don't abandon faith. Keep on believing what you originally believed God for! The lesson is that fear robs you of what you originally wanted from God. Fear aborts victories, fear aborts blessings. Fear destroys destinies.

When Jesus says, "The damsel is sleeping, not dead," He takes authority over Satan and death by refusing to accept the finality of the words the messenger and the evidence of wailing and crying that he sees at Jairus's house. The next passage reads, "Straightaway the damsel arose and walked," which shows us that faith always triumphs. Persistence pays. A focus on God and his word is the key to victory.

I tucked Pastor Chimunda's words away into my heart. My friend, Lee McClure, told me that God, in his perfect wisdom, was adding to my story and I tucked that into my heart, too. I had more tests run for MS—MRIs, blood work, whatever needed to be done. The MRI showed many lesions on my brain, so I was sent to a neurologist.

The neurologist had me do four more hours of MRIs because my Primary Care Physician reported that I had active lesions. Waiting for the test results in her office, I kept praying under my breath for no new lesions. *Nothing new God!* When the doctor came in, she had technology problems and had difficulty pulling up the results. She left the room to get a different computer and you could have heard a pin drop. I felt like it was all in slow motion. I was still praying under my breath, and I was having a strong conversation with the enemy. When the doctor returned, she came back in and confirmed numerous lesions on my brain and spine. But these were just old lesions. There were no new lesions. I began to pray again, this time with praise. *Thank you, God, thank you God!* I wanted to run and sing and cry and just bow on my knees to my God. *My faithful God.* The enemy was trying to steal my story, to steal my message, but God was taking it back: I HAD NO NEW LESIONS BECAUSE I AM HEALED!

Blakely's Story

Throughout my journey of healing, I have learned that things are not always as they seem. I could have let this totally devastate me because of all the symptoms and doctor reports saying the MS was active. I was determined to not let go of my belief, it was what I had to do.

It reminds me of a story about my grand-daughter, Blakely Reese. She is named after my son, Blake, and has been a joy since Day 1. One weekend close to Christmas, she and her family were visiting with us when she decided that she wanted to have a Christmas party out in the backyard storage house with Harper. I helped them decorate and helped them make refreshments to make it seem like a big deal. Blakely—who has an entrepreneurial spirit—decided she wanted to make a little money, so she charged $2 per person to get in the door. All the adults laughed and dug into their pockets to pay up. My son and daughter-in-law paid four $1 bills, but Chelsea and her husband, Jordan, gave her two bills—a $5 bill, and a $1 bill. A few minutes later, Blakely called me over to the corner and said, "Nana, we have a problem. You need to tell Chelsea and Jordan they did not pay enough to get in. I need $4 and they only gave me $2."

Blakely wasn't old enough to understand that she had more than enough money from Chelsea and Jordan, because she only saw two bills in her hand. This is a perfect illustration of how the way that things look and the way that we perceive them can be deceiving. Blakely didn't understand how to count that money, but this was a great opportunity to show her how.

To have a clear understanding in our lives of God's reality, we need not be quick to judge and we need to stay in prayer for discernment. We need God to teach us the truth, just as I needed to teach Blakely the truth. When I started to worry about my healing from MS, I stayed in prayer for discernment, and I waited for God to show me the truth.

Use Your Mess for Your Message

Through my experiences with MS, I became more confident in my beliefs than ever before. My BELIEF was strengthened to a new level. I wanted to sing from the mountain top. Everything that God takes us through is something we can use for our message. I love that Joyce Meyers talks about using your pain for gain in her study Bible by encouraging us to let our mess be our message and our ministry (p. 2038). God needs experienced help, the same as an employer looking to hire a new employee needs experienced help. When we go to work for God in his kingdom, He will use everything we have experienced in our past, no matter how painful it was for us. He considers our pain to be experience. By our experiences, we are qualified to take someone else through them too. **Hebrews 5:8-9** tells us that even Jesus gained experience through the things that He suffered, so if you have pain in your past, know that it can be used for good in God's Kingdom and let this encourage you.

I heard this quotation one day by writer, Andy Andrews, that permeated my heart because it reminds us of our proof of hope. This proof of hope is one of the most powerful bridges to the lives of other people in our lives. Andrews writes, "Even in the worst time of life, if you are still breathing, that means you are still alive. If you are still here, you haven't accomplished what is still to be accomplished. The most important part of your life is still ahead of you."

This statement tells me that there is so much ahead of me, and I should be excited to still be here. There is still a lot for me to do, more people to help and more lessons to learn. This quotation is one of those things you never forget. For instance, your mom's homemade chocolate pie, or your favorite hat from your favorite uncle. It is something memorable, that will be with you forever. My message is about hope, and it is also about you gathering your armor to GO in obedience to do what God has called you to do, even when you encounter adversity. Even if you have been rejected. Even if you don't feel loved. Even if you were abused. Even if you messed up again and again. Even if...

REFLECTION POINTS

- Hold strong to your faith and God's promises
- Lean INTO God when circumstances cause confusion
- Things are not always as they seem
- You are still breathing

Chapter 3
Blake's Crash—His Flight to Heaven

I never thought I would be a parent that had to bury a child. But I did, and with God's help, I not only survived a horrible ordeal, I found peace and an even stronger relationship with Him. I had always thought that burying a child was something that I could never do. I thought that I could have never survived it and that I would not want to if I did. But I was thrown into the reality of it and I went into numbness, walking through the motions, planning a celebration service, even though, in my heart, I couldn't celebrate. My mind was going a million miles an hour and I kept praying for God to wake me up. *This MUST be a dream. Wake me up! God, please! This can't be happening. The pain is indescribable.*

Blake was my first-born son. He was adventurous, he was full of life, he had a kind heart, and he had dreams early in his high school years to be a pilot. He was very active in sports—he played basketball, played racket ball, skied, and snowboarded—he was a very good athlete. However, from the time he was a little boy, he wanted to fly. I have pictures of him, from when he was little, in which he's holding a plane in his hand, playing. As he grew older, he loved the farmer's life. Much like his dad—who was also a farmer—he was a 6'4" slender guy. When Blake was little, he would go with his dad to change water, move pipe, play in the ditch, and ride the tractor. He loved that life. He knew he didn't want to go to college but wanted to put his effort and time into being a commercial pilot. He wanted to be a crop duster. He got his pilot's license when he was a sophomore and, after he graduated high school, he finished up his training hours to get his commercial license so that he could begin working. He was determined to make it happen.

Blake married Molly a few years later and kept going with his flying career. He had so many mentors and friends who taught him and helped him to reach his goal to become a pilot. We were so proud of him, but if I am honest, the flying did make me nervous. I prayed a lot for his protection. Blake had a friend, Jeremy Barnett, and he lived outside of Clovis. They were very close and spent some great time together. Every morning, Blake would fly over Jeremy's home on the way to his work. Jeremy's kids would come out of the house and Blake would wave at them with the plane. When Blake's sister, Chelsea, was back in Clovis, he would take her flying. He would take me up and one day he flew us over Lake Alan Henry so that we could see the lake. It was a little windy, but it was so fun to ride with him and see how he handled the plane. He took it very seriously.

Special Moments

Have you ever looked back on your life to see the ways that God gifted you special moments with the ones you love just before their death? One month before Blake's crash, I made a last-minute decision to visit my mother for the weekend. When I got there, Blake and his wife, Molly, invited us to a 100-year Reunion for the church I grew up in, First Baptist Church in Bovina. Of course, we wanted to go, so my mom and I spent several quality hours with them that whole weekend. I watched him cook on the grill with the men from the church, and I watched him serve everyone around him. It was such a special weekend and little did I know it would be the last time I saw Blake.

That Sunday morning when I left, I stopped by to see him during church on the way to the airport. He came outside to give me his big bear hug, which he is famous for. His 6'4" height and that super thin physique will never be forgotten. His arms could reach around me almost one-and-a-half times. Everyone loved his hugs. I remember the new shirt he was wearing; I remember the hug. I drove away, waving bye, not knowing it would be the last time I would see him face to face.

That Fateful Day

On Friday, September 12, 2003, I went to work like any other day. I remember it was a dreary, rainy day. I had no idea my life was about to change. I remember specifically looking at the time on my computer at 9:01 and thinking, "Hmmm;" it was like I stared at it for a moment in a daze, then went about my work. In the next hour, everything I knew as normal was no longer normal. I specifically recall every event that took place. My husband had to drive 30 minutes to get to me and he was speeding across the metroplex, hoping to get there before I got a call from someone else or found out on my own. God was with him all the way.

My boss came to my desk and smugly told me to follow her. She turned and walked down a long hallway. She would not look at me; she just kept walking. I wondered if I was about to get fired. *What in the world had I done?* I had no idea. She took me to a conference room, I walked in, and there on the right side of the table was my pastor and a visiting pastor from the previous Sunday's service. On the left side was Tommy. The only way Tommy knew to tell me was direct. In tears, he said, "Blake had a crash, and he is gone."

My world stopped. That next 45 minutes in that room were filled with tears, wailing, kicking the table underneath me as I sat and cried. I could not accept it; my heart was broken into a million pieces. I remember saying to my pastor, "I did not pray for his protection last night! I was going to call him last night and I didn't!"

The guilt kicked in. It was gut-wrenching. I hurt all over. To this day, 18 years later, the afternoon is still very clear to me.

God's Faithfulness

God started showing His faithfulness to us before we even got in the car at my work to go to the house. A sister called to tell me that someone told her they had seen Blake in church on Wednesday night and that he was worshiping God with his arms raised. He was 6'4" and she said if he could reach two more inches, he would have been in heaven then. It gave me a beautiful picture of my son, loving on God.

My younger son, Scott, lived close to Blake. He knew what had happened. I called him on the way home in the car, but I couldn't even understand him through the tears and anguish in his voice. I wanted to be with him, to hold him, to cry with him. We had to go get Chelsea at school and Tommy did not want us to both go in, he thought it would scare her. When they walked out of the school, Chelsea kept on asking what was wrong. *What had happened?* Tommy finally stopped in the rain, and told her, and she fell to the ground. I was in the car and ran out to her. The three of us stood in the rain, just holding on to each other. All our hearts were in a million pieces now and breaking more and more. We were in disbelief. It was too much. I remember how Chelsea was locked into a stare on the way home and could not move. My mom, who had only come to see us one time in the 18 years that we had lived in Dallas area, was with us. This was, again, the work of God. I needed my mom and my mom needed me.

Later that day, one of Blake's best friends told me they had played golf earlier that week and Blake had told him that his life was so perfect. He told him that it was almost scary how perfect it was. I have never had anyone tell me that before, that their life was so perfect.

In fact, a year before, his life was not so perfect. I remember one night stepping outside and leaning over our safety fence around our pool, in the dark, stars shining, and praying for Molly and him. Their walk with God had gone astray and they had been on a different path. I prayed specifically that God would put someone in their path to draw them closer to Him, and that is exactly what happened. It was not how I had pictured it, but the end result drew Blake and Molly back to God, and to each other, in an even stronger way. There is nothing that can be more precious for a mother than to know that their children love the Lord and will spend their lives in eternity with the Father.

Throughout the next few days, God continued to show himself faithful. Our family was walking through the motions, but God just loved on us and spoke to us. On the way to the funeral home, God gave me a vision. I was in the front seat of the car, bent over, crying, wondering if Blake knew he was going to die, thinking: *what happened, is this real???* The vision was of a large angel wing, swooshing across me. In that moment, it felt like a strong breeze crossed my face. God spoke to me and said, "I had him before he hit the ground." I pictured Blake above the scene of the accident, being held by the angel. He had him before he hit the ground. What a relief for the moment; that image got me through the next few days.

So many people loved Blake, so many came to the house, so many came to his celebration service. It was standing room only and our friends told us that the church looked like a Thomas Kincaid painting before the service. It was perfect. Blake's friends who flew with him did a 'missing man formation' fly by at the graveside, with one plane separating off from the others to represent a good-bye from Blake.

God continued to show us his faithfulness when we got home a week later. I went back to work a week after that. I knew that if I stayed home in an empty house, I would just relive the entire event over and over. The third day after my return to work, I left my office at lunch and went to a Christian bookstore. I needed something from God. I walked in and there, in front of me, inside the door, was a 16x20 picture of a large angel with a huge wing spread over a little boy in his bed. The scripture at the bottom of the picture is **Psalm 91:11**, "He will give His angels charge over you to watch you in all your ways." This was more confirmation and peace for me to carry in my heart in the days to come.

Breaking My Fall, Jeremy Camp

Molly, our daughter-in-law, called when she went to the farm to get Blake's truck, where he had last parked it. In his CD player, she found a disc by Jeremy Camp set to the song, "Breaking My Fall." I did not know who Jeremy Camp was, but soon found out and bought the CD. He is a well known American contemporary Christian music singer and songwriter. I remember praying to God to please let me meet Jeremy Camp one day so I could ask him about that song. A few years later, when I was not expecting it, God brought that to fruition.

One day at work, I was listening to the radio, and they announced there would be a private concert with Jeremy Camp in the metroplex. The radio station would be announcing different locations where we could pick up tickets but they would not announce the location until the day of the concert. Because I was working, I could not be at the specific places at specific times to get the tickets, but I was NOT going to miss this opportunity to talk to Jeremy. I decided to call into the radio station. I explained to them my story about Blake and told them that I really needed to be at the concert. They put me on hold and came back with 10 tickets that they put on hold for me at the concert.

The morning of the concert, the radio station hosted an interview with Jeremy and opened calls at the end to talk to him. I started dialing and dialing and dialing. *Busy—busy—busy.* Then, "HELLO?"—I was terrified to talk to him—"Hello, this is Jeremy Camp." Little did I know I was on 'live' radio. Talk about stuttering. Speaking with him, I shared my story, and he told me why he wrote the song. It was written after his wife of four months, died from cancer. He was devastated. At first, he did okay after her death, walking through the motions. However, after the first few months he felt himself starting to fall and he didn't know what to do. He called out to God, and this was the spark he used to write this song. In the song, he talks about crying out to God because he was falling. He asked God, "What am I supposed to do?" It makes me wonder if Blake did the same, as his plane was going down. Was he calling out to God, asking Him to break his fall?

Jeremy asked me if I was coming to the concert, and of course, I said "Yes!" He told me to wait after the concert to talk with him. *What????? Where is the location????* *Please!! I was living in the Dallas Metroplex at the time, so the concert could have been ANYWHERE!* When they announced the location, it was ON MY ROUTE HOME off a side street at a beautiful small church. *Really? How can that be? For real?* I just could not believe it! God was faithful again—it just amazed me.

That night, Tommy, Chelsea, and I attended the concert. We got there early and stood in line in the cold, rainy weather wrapped in blankets. The doors finally opened, and we walked into the church with a crowd, but then located our amazing seats, not too far from the front of the sanctuary. I was pinching myself as I tried to believe this was all happening. Afterwards, we waited until the crowd had gotten their new CDs and left. Suddenly, it was my turn to speak to Jeremy. I stepped up and told Jeremy who I was. He was so kind and talked with me for a bit. He told me more about the song, "Breaking My Fall," and autographed extra CDs for my family. I will forever be grateful for his heart in helping us heal. I walked out of that little church on cloud nine!

God's Promises to Remember

There were so many passages that God showed me throughout this part of my journey as I sought Him. I believe that is the key—we must seek Him to find him. I could not pray, because I did not know what to pray *for*. I was in a slump for most of that first year, however, after a time, I started getting back into the word and finding scripture to give me peace and to give me hope. Some of the scripture that helped me and can help you, are as follows:

1. **Ps 46:1**. God is our refuge and our strength, an ever-present help in times of trouble. (The day my life changed)
2. **Ps 31:24**. Be strong and take heart, all you who hope in the Lord. (Messages I got same day as Blake's crash)
3. **2 Cor 4:16-18**. Therefore, we do not lose heart. Though, outwardly we are wasting away, yet inwardly we are being renewed day by day. For our light and momentary troubles are achieving for us an eternal glory that far outweighs them all. So, we fix our eyes on not what is seen, but what is unseen. For what is seen is temporary, but what is unseen is eternal. (Angel vision)
4. **2 Cor. 12:9**. But he said to me, my grace is sufficient for you, for my power is make perfect in your weakness. (The service, the fly by)
5. **Josh 1:9**. Be strong and courageous! Don't be afraid or discouraged. For the Lord your God is with you wherever you go. (Going back to work 1 week later)

6. **Ps 91:11**. He will give his angels charge over you to watch you in all your ways. Christian Bookstore, picture of angel (confirmed Angel vision).
7. **Rom 12:12**. Rejoice in Hope, be patient in affliction and be constant in prayer.) (I could not pray)
8. **Ex 14:13**. The Lord will fight for you. You Need only to be still. (I wanted to go to be with Blake, God's Grace, I am here for a reason)

And the list goes on. I have many scriptures and promises that got me through this time. God's faithfulness makes me so aware of the big events in my life, and the little ones. His Strength IN ME got me through. I just kept believing that He would show me what was next with our new normal. It took time.

More Loss, More Pain!

This fall season of 2003 was a horrible time for our family. My father-in-law unexpectedly passed away on Nov. 6th, 1 ½ months after Blake. It was too much to process for us all. My uncle Bob and aunt Mary came down from Colorado for the funeral service. After dark, my uncle wanted to take a walk for a bit to get some fresh air and, before he left, I told him, jokingly, "If you are gone more than 30 minutes, we are coming to find you." "Okay," he answered, "but I will be back." And can you guess what happened next? He didn't come home, and I sent Molly to look for him. Molly had just lost her husband, my son. She came upon the scene of an accident, to find that Bob had walked into a busy street, gotten hit by a car, and died before he got to the hospital. *WAIT, WHAT?* We had just been at my in-laws' home visiting with family and friends, remembering my dear father-in-law. Now we were on the way to the hospital because Bob has been hit by a car. "Please God!" I prayed "Nothing else, I can't take this!" I was so numb from losing Blake that I could not deal with this too. And poor Tommy; he was trying to be there for me, his mother, and his sisters while dealing with his own heart. I remember him sobbing at his dad's service and shaking, but I could do nothing to help him. I was still having difficulty believing my son was gone.

A couple of years earlier, my little sister, Tammy, had lost her 15-year-old daughter, Nancy Roxanne. She told me, "Everyone deals with their grief different. Anything goes, as long as you don't want to hurt yourself or someone else." That helped me so much, because I did think I was going crazy sometimes when I curled up into a ball in my bedroom at night, alone and crying. I wanted to be with Blake! I kept thinking that I would never get out of my own head. All I could think about was Blake's loss and my missing him all the time. But, as God would have it, time has helped me heal. The hole in my heart will never be filled, but God's love has restored us over and again.

Releasing Emotions

I have never been a crier, however, I cried so much when Blake left us. I did a lot of it in private. One day, I was reading in Nehemiah 1:4, "When I heard this, I sat down and wept and mourned for days and fasted and prayed before the God of heaven." Nehemiah was not afraid to weep unashamedly. Some people won't show emotions or weep, but when you don't release these emotions, your emotions can eat away at you on the inside. God gave us tear glands; we need to weep. I encourage you to take this scripture to heart and let your emotions go when you need to cry.

One More Story
How God Kept Showing His Love

My birthday is in October, and Blake left us in September. On my birthday, the doorbell rang and I received the most beautiful flowers you have ever seen. Not your normal flower arrangement, but the most magnificent, unique, and colorful one. There was a card that said "Happy Birthday—Love you" without a signature. I called the flower shop, and they did not have a name. They said the sender wanted to remain anonymous. I was emotional and I called my family, sisters, brother, Tommy, and Tommy's family, but no; they had not sent them. Suddenly, I had all kinds of thoughts going through my head. *Who are these from? Are they from Blake? Did he somehow send these to me from heaven?*

Jeremy's The One

Several years later, I was visiting my mom in Clovis, NM and I called Blake's friend, Jeremy. This was the Jeremy with the family that Blake waved at every morning as he flew his plane over their house. We met for coffee and talked and loved on each other. He is such a special young man, and I will forever love him. Somehow, the flowers came up in the conversation and I told him I could not figure out who had sent them. Suddenly, I could tell by his body language and reaction that HE WAS THE ONE! He did admit it after a bit, and he told me this, "Blake would have wanted me to send you flowers for him on your birthday every year." He told me he would continue to send me flowers for as long as he is alive and he has followed through on that promise even as we've moved from three different addresses in the Dallas Area and three different places in Lubbock. It is amazing how he has done that without my knowing, but he has been consistent for 18 years.

Take This Away

In sharing my story here, I hope to encourage you by reminding you that, because you are still here, you can have hope. God is faithful. Dig deep and get familiar with His word and his promises; His word that does not return void. Ask God to show you what He has for you, and then walk in that truth. The things you go through can be a catalyst for passion in your heart. In the next chapter, you will see where my passion grew and how I used that passion to share about God's faithfulness and to give others hope.

REFLECTION POINTS

- God is faithful.
- You are never without Hope if you are still here.
- Be still, allow God to show you His love.
- Always make that phone call or say that prayer; you never know if it will be the last.

Chapter 4
Passion Born

What is This Passion?

I was in my 30s before I really knew my purpose/passion. My life stories have built my passion and designed my purpose. I am not an expert to teach about passion and purpose, but my belief is that before you can find your purpose, you first need to find your passion. We can sometimes get complacent with life, just thinking *it is what it is. There is nothing I can do about the place I'm in,* but if you're feeling this way I think it is possible that you've lost sight of who God made you to be and what He designed you to do. Charles Stanley has shared several lessons regarding passion and purpose. He says that there are two truths you must face up to if you truly want to pursue your purpose and reach your full potential in life.

- **TRUTH #1.** God has placed more within you than you realize.

- **TRUTH #2.** You likely have settled for the life you're living now.

When God looks at you, He sees all of the awesome potential and possibilities He has created you to fulfill. Stanley also says that if you're willing to discover and align yourself with God's plan and purpose for you, He'll bless you more than you could ever imagine and open doors of opportunity you never dreamed possible. He'll restore the joy, peace, and the hope you've lost and show you the path to what He wants you to accomplish in your life. And he promises to bless you with life at its very best.

I taught a group of women leaders in Dallas about passion in 2014. This was an opportunity to join together with powerful women who wanted more in their walk with the Lord, and who also wanted to use what they had learned to pay it forward to others. I chose to talk about passion, and, in diving into some studies before my talk, I learned that once a woman understands her identity in Christ, she should begin exploring what makes her unique. This exploration may be a lifelong process of self-discovery. When you land upon a goldmine of passion, though, you will find an endless supply of energy and purpose in your life. Let's talk about what passion is.

Passion: Your zeal in life and the fuel that enables you to change the world. True passion will pull you towards your destiny.

Most people experience three different kinds of passion in life.

- *PERSONAL PASSION*

  Personal passions are often the easiest passions to identify because it's so easy to hear our (sometimes) self-absorbed voices tell us what we want, need, or deserve. I am passionate about Mexican food, painting, and journaling. Painting and journaling can be healthy and help me connect with God and recharge before I see other people, but too much Mexican food can impact my health. In other words, we must learn to develop our personal passions without becoming absorbed in them.

- *GENERAL PASSION*

  General passion, on the other hand, is about empathy for others. We experience general passion when we're watching the news and a story about the plight of a group or an individual strikes a deep chord of emotion within us and we might think, *Somebody should do something about this!* Many of us experienced general passion when we witnessed the events of 9/11, for example, or—more recently—when 13 soldiers were killed in Afghanistan. General passion doesn't always move you to the point of action, but you sure want someone else to do something about it.

- *GENUINE PASSION—MY FOCUS*

This passion moves you to the point of saying, "I must do something about this, I must make a difference." The cliché for genuine passion might go, "If it's going to be, it's up to me." I believe that our purpose is rooted in genuine passion.

There are two main groups of people who experience this kind of passion.

1. The first group is filled with people whose passion is built into them. Like an un-anchored boat, their life has moved by an invisible force in the general direction of an internal desire. I think of how, as a young man, Bill Gates had already begun developing games himself and had begun building his own computer programs and business at the age of 15. Similarly, Michael Jordan loved sports and he was very competitive at an early age. In games, he never gave up, even though there were times that he wanted to. Sports were in his DNA.

2. The second group is filled with people who have had experiences in life thrust upon them that created deep-rooted emotional pain. They want to help eliminate this pain in the lives of other people.

My Daughter

My daughter, Chelsea, was always passionate about school and she did well in it. She had a general passion to meet her mate and get married (and she did), then when she finished up college, she started teaching. She taught middle school and some high school, but soon decided it was not something she wanted to continue to do.

Instead of quitting, she decided to push forward and get her master's degree to become a school counselor. Now, she is a College Advisor, helping students to get grants, scholarships, and to learn what is available to them. Most of the students have no idea what is available for them in terms of a college education. One day last year, she called me up in tears. She had just called two of her seniors to give them the news that they had been awarded full-ride college scholarships. The students cried and Chelsea did, too, so I asked her why she was emotional. She told me that she loved helping these kids. This was something she had to do; she loved making a difference in their lives while expecting nothing in return. She has developed her passion through life experiences.

Sally's Story

I have a friend, Sally (I've changed her name to protect her identity), who was homeless at an early age and experienced a lot of trauma—including drug addiction, incarceration, and being shuffled around among four different families—before she was 12 years old. In her teen years, she ran around the streets, sometimes even using a bird bath to clean herself up. In her early 20s, she was invited to a church group where she found out about God and how much He loved her. Because of all the love that He showed her, she wanted to pour that love out to others, so she focused on helping broken people who were experiencing the same things that she had experienced. She asked for volunteers to help her with donations of food and blankets for those who were homeless and in need. That was just the beginning, though. She now has a ministry helping the homeless. Someone even donated a building in Ft. Worth, Texas to support her mission of helping others. From her experiences of pain, her *passion* has become her *purpose.*

How I Developed My Passion

I have developed my passion and purpose through my life experiences. I buried a child, feared the unknown with Multiple Sclerosis, lost my voice, divorced my first husband, and felt my entire body shut down in 2020. In each of these circumstances, I wanted to help others going through the same things that I had. I wanted to empower them to push forward and find their calling. I wanted to give hope to people who didn't have hope and to help them understand what is inside of them that God wants to use. I wanted them to know that God is faithful and that they have the capacity to do whatever He has called them to do. I wanted them to see and understand to Whom they really belonged so that they could accept the love Jesus had for them.

To help you find your own passion and purpose, I encourage you to do these four things:
1. Begin with what you know.
2. Make choices based on what you like and what you know. Likes could turn into passions, but they may start as interests.
3. Make some choices based on what really bugs you (what you dislike).
4. When you find something that you want to change or something you want to be a part of, you're getting closer to your passion.

If finding your passion is something you struggle with, I also want to encourage you to spend some time with God and to seek his guidance through his word. When it comes to this subject of passion and what God helps us to do, the following Scripture is an excellent resource, "He comes along aside us when we go through hard times, and before you know it, he brings us alongside someone else who is going through hard times so that we can be there for them just as God was there for us." **1 Cor. 1-4**. (Msg)

In praying about my own passion, God helped me create the following acronym:

Press In

Ask for Clarity

Spend Time in Prayer

Soak in His Presence

Identify with Purpose

Open Mind

Never, Never Give Up on Your Passion

To sum the acronym up, **P**ress into God, **A**sk Him for clarity as you **S**pend time in prayer. **S**oak in His presence while seeking guidance that helps you **I**dentify with your purpose. Be **O**pen minded and **N**ever, never, never give up on your passion. Once you determine what your passion is, your life will change because you will know your purpose.

Jesus knew His purpose and this impacted how He lived His life. In **John 10:10**, Jesus said that He "came into the world that we might have life." In **John 18:37**, He told Pilate, "This is why I was born, and for this I have come into the world, to bear witness to the Truth." John wrote that Jesus's purpose was to destroy the works of the devil and that is what he did.

We All Need Purpose

When we don't have a purpose in life, we can feel useless, worthless, and frustrated, so it is very important for us to learn that God has designed us with a purpose in mind. (**Psalm 139:16**). We are all different, and we all have a different passion to couple with our purpose. Many of you may be in a season right now in which you are in transition and uncertain what to do next, but God will show you.

Finding our purpose requires taking steps of faith, however. In her Study Bible, Joyce Meyer writes that stepping out into the unknown and launching out into the deep water can be frightening (p. 1612). Fear can get the best of us and many people miss God's will for their lives because they play it safe. But *Better safe than sorry* does not always work in God's economy. If we tried to be safe all the time, we would not be where God wants us to be. To fulfill our purpose in life, we must ask God to make clear what He wants us to do and then obey Him. When God calls us to do something, we need to do it. We need to move forward to answer that call. We need to pray to God each step of the way for guidance and protection and confirmation that we are on the right path.

REFLECTION POINTS

- Life experiences can help you develop your passion
- Jesus knew His purpose (**John 10:10**)

Chapter 5
G.R.A.C.E.

Years ago, I was going through a tough time when God gave me an acronym for GRACE. Over the years, I have taught this message to women's groups in small settings. Even though I know that God's grace is sufficient and immeasurable, this message is ultimately about obedience.

In 2014, my husband, Tommy, and I were living in the Dallas area when we took a trip back home to Clovis, NM for a long weekend with family. I had had some pretty life-changing thoughts going through my mind on my way back home and wanted to talk to Tommy about what was on my heart.

I had always had a job and, most of that time, I was also an entrepreneur and business owner. I have an entrepreneurial spirit. I love starting businesses and making connections with people and I love giving them opportunities to start their own businesses. At that time, I felt strongly in my heart that I needed to quit my job and work at replacing my six-figure income with my other business I owned. My business was not earning me anywhere near that kind of income, but I truly believed I could do it.

Tommy, on the other hand was not supportive of the idea at all and, looking back, I can totally understand why. He is very much a pessimist and realist. We are opposite—glass half full (me), and glass half empty (him). We were a hard-working couple with a daughter at home. We had a mortgage payment, car payments, credit card bills, school, and many other expenses. For me to quit my job with a great income did not make sense to him. I had been doing both for some time now, so he wanted me to continue doing the same.

The conversation got heated, and I looked up as we were driving through a small town called Boyd, TX. I remember it like it was yesterday, it had an impact. We were passing a church and they had a marquis with this message: 'The Grace of God is Immeasurable.' I could not get that message out of my head and when I got home, I dove into a study on Grace. I love the fact that God's grace is Immeasurable (limitless). While I was in deep thought about this short message from that little marquis, God, in his amazing ways, gave me an acronym for Grace that continues to stick with me today and I use it often, teaching and for myself.

As He gave me the acronym, I started looking up each word with the definition, and wow! The lessons I will share in this book that tie into each of these words will bless you and will hopefully help you to get on a path to use them in your life. The acronym is as follows:

Go
Reckless
Abandon
Confident
Expectation

In stating this all together it would sound like this: **'Go in Reckless Abandon with Confident Expectation.'** Below, I've tied the definitions of each of these words together.

Definitions

- **Go**—depart, just go, be in motion, be obedient
- **Reckless**—go without paying attention to circumstances, just going to a target, blinders on, don't look to left or to the right
- **Abandon**—Yield completely to what God wants to do, get out of your comfort zone, freedom from restraint
- **Confident**—strong belief, full assurance, no uncertainty
- **Expectation**—Looking forward to, anticipating

The message is this: Just go. Regardless of circumstances, go to your target, don't focus on your past, blinders on, eyes straight ahead, no questioning. Get out of your comfort zone, yielding completely. Be strong in your belief and anticipate great things to come.

God will bless your obedience. Even though Tommy and I disagreed at that time, I ultimately decided to quit my job and just Go.

Breaking It Down

GO

In **Genesis 12:1**, God tells Abraham, "Leave your country, your family and your father's home for a land that I will show you. God asks Abraham to leave his comfort zone without knowing where he is going." He then says, "I'll make you a great nation and bless you," meaning, "I'll make you famous, you'll be a blessing. I'll bless those who bless you; those who curse you I'll curse. All the families of the Earth will be blessed through you." These promises from God support Abraham's decision to go. He knows blessings will come and those who curse him will be taken out of his way.

Abraham was 75 years old! In verse 3, Abram left just as God said (**Gen 26: 3-6**). In **Gen 35:1-3**, God told Isaac to stay so that he would receive the blessing from Abraham's obedience, so Isaac stayed! In **Gen 25: 1-25**, God told Jacob to go back to Bethel and Jacob went back. In **Josh 1:2-3**, God told Joshua to get going and to keep up the mission that Moses had started during his lifetime. He promised that he would give him every square inch of the land he set his feet on, just like he promised. Joshua gave orders to all the leaders to *pack their bags* because they were leaving. Joshua had the obedience to go! And the blessings followed, as they still do today.

Can you recall times you have stepped out and started something, only to quit? Quitting can lead you to experience all kinds of beliefs and emotions, but quitting does not mean *failure*. Quitting can be a learning experience if you choose to look ahead. I want to share a few stories of my own experiences stepping out and share the ways that God has shown up for me.

My Evan Story

Evan was a great friend of mine whom I knew through business. He was always joking around and loved everyone. He was very proud of his career helping to assist couples with their weddings and he was very smart. He made us laugh and was so fun to be around. Evan was sick with AIDS, however, and I watched his health decline over the couple of years I knew him.

Evan was raised Jewish and there were several things he was very curious about regarding Christianity. I had witnessed to him, and he had a lot of questions for me. He had a few people in his life that he expressed this to. I am trusting God that Evan had a peace about this prior to his death.

When the day came that he left us, I was surprised to learn from Evan's best friend that Evan wanted me to do his graveside service. I had spoken at my mother-in-law's service, and Evan wanted me to lead his service alongside a rabbi. I did not know anyone in Evan's Chicago family, and I had surely never been in this position before, but I wanted to honor Evan's wishes. The whole event led me to experience a lot of emotion and nervousness regarding how his family would receive my message at the graveside since we didn't share beliefs. I decided to GO with confident expectation, knowing God would be by my side.

As I stood beside the grave, Evan's family got out of their cars together with the rabbi. Their heads were covered and no one was talking. There were no flowers, as they represent happiness and life. I was asked to speak first, and I painted a picture in which I celebrated Evan's life based on the time I knew him, including all the great things he had done for people. He was a servant, he was funny, he was optimistic, and he was incredibly creative. My stories made the people who knew him laugh. I prayed at the end, and then the rabbi did the second half of the service. I just listened with interest trying to understand that part of the culture to which he was acclimated. I realized how much I had not understood and how much I needed to learn.

That afternoon, we had a gathering with all his family and local friends and, after a while, his brother and sister came to me asked me to come into a separate hall to talk with them. I was a bit concerned—and curious—because I had no idea how they felt about what I presented at the graveside. I was hoping I had not offended them in any way. God, in His faithful way, came through again by honoring my obedience. His family expressed to me they were very pleased with how everything went and told me that it could not have been more perfect. They were so appreciative for the help and the way that I painted the picture of Evan, our friend. They felt that my stories had been edifying to his memory and they had served as a way to express how his friends here loved him. This can only be explained as God's covering because I had accepted the invitation to GO!

My Starbucks Story

On another morning, God told me to GO once again when I was praying and journaling. I had been asking God to allow me to hear Him more clearly and to help me step out in bravery to do what He was asking me to do. At that time, I had become familiar with a youth group who had been doing ministry on the streets and this group always prayed for God to show them who they needed to minister to. God had always shown them faithfully who needed prayer and so many blessings came from this obedience.

As I prayed that morning and journaled, I felt God telling me to go to Starbucks and to look for someone in a purple shirt and glasses. "Really?" I thought, "I am courageous but I have never done anything like this."

I put my trip to Starbucks off all day long but finally chose to walk in obedience. I went in to Starbucks, ordered a drink, and sat at a table. I started looking around the room, but no one was wearing a purple shirt and glasses. A couple walked in, and a man was wearing a purple shirt. As I thought about asking to pray for him though, I realized he did not have glasses. I needed to wait, so I sat and waited.

Just as I was getting ready to leave, the door opened again and a lady walked through that door wearing a purple shirt and glasses. I sat there for a moment and then my fear kicked in. *What was she going to think? She would think I was crazy! What was I going to say to her? My goodness!* What in the world am I doing? However, I wanted this badly enough, to be obedient and watch God work. I knew He would bless my obedience, even if this lady needed nothing! I walked over to her and said, "Hello, my name is Nancy. You may think I am crazy, but I was praying this morning and God told me that I needed to be here to pray with someone. Is there anything I can pray with you about?"

This lady started weeping and said, "I can't believe this." Just then a friend of hers came in and sat with her at the table. I was still standing. They asked me to sit with them. The lady was having marital problems, and some big things had happened to her recently, and she was hopeless. I asked them if I could pray, and we held hands and prayed.

When I left, I realized that I did not have to worry about the results; I just had to be obedient. It was a lesson for me to follow through. It gave me confidence to remain aware of the people around me and listen to that still, small voice inviting me to pray for people when I felt led. I have only had one person over the years tell me, no and I am okay with that, because I know it is a big responsibility to follow through when you ask God for something, and He gives you direction.

My Mom's Story

In May 2015, Tommy and I moved to the Texas Panhandle to be closer to our kids and granddaughters. We built a home with an extra master suite, so that we would have plenty of room for guests when they came to visit. Little did we know that in January of 2016 we would be moving my mother in with us due to her declining health. None of my siblings were in a place in their lives that they could take her in, so Tommy and I quickly decided that we would move her in with us. It came as a shock to her because she did not want to leave the independence of her home and the freedom of her car, but we could not allow her to be unsafe. She had had too many falls and it was too dangerous to leave her alone. None of us lived in the same town as she did, and it would take us two hours to get to her. She also had shown early symptoms of dementia, so there was no question that we had to make that decision for her.

Knowing how she felt, taking her in was a tough decision. She was mad. She was sad. She cried a lot. She would shut her bedroom door and not come out for long periods. It was so hard. However, we knew God directed us to take care of her and that it was the right thing to do.

I reached out to Norman, our pastor in Dallas, and he referred me to the Bible with specific scripture regarding taking care of the elderly and the blessings that would come from obeying God's word. It truly gave us peace of mind, and we also knew we were on the right track. She was with us only a few months when she fell and broke her left femur while on a trip with family to see the bluebonnets. She had to go for rehab in a nursing home after her surgery and she was never able to come back home, even though we sincerely wanted her with us. We would visit often, and at least four days a week, I would have coffee and spend time with her on my way to work. When COVID hit, that all changed. First, I got sick for a few weeks, and she was worried about me because I was not coming anymore. Then COVID locked down the nursing homes, so that she couldn't have visitors. With her progressing dementia, this was heart-wrenching.

Her move was tough at first and it was not an easy task to be responsible for her. I had to take her to doctor appointments, where I loaded and unloaded her wheelchair. I listened to her complaints and, at times, I became tired and frustrated with her. But the blessings that came from taking care of her have been amazing. The memories I made with my mom are so special to me. I will never be able to replace the times when we had coffee, read a daily devotional, prayed and laughed together. Over time, I watched how she built relationships with the people at the nursing facility. Everyone was her friend, and everyone wanted to be around her. She was kind, caring, compassionate towards them all. I realized that my passion for relationships comes from her and for that, I will be forever grateful.

The three stories above are only a few of the stories that I had on my heart as I was writing, but they all clearly make my point about being obedient and just going and doing what God tells you to do. They illustrate how you can put your blinders on, free from the restrain of fear, to get yourself out of your comfort zone. When do you recall obeying God and how did God bless those acts?

Reckless Abandon with Confident Expectation

Being Reckless and totally putting your blinders on to allow God to have complete control takes intentional commitment and prayer. And it takes obedience to follow through. Let's dive into being reckless and putting your blinders on. Trusting God is one of the things I have had to learn to do over the years. These stories would have gone a different way if I had just done my own thing without knowing God would bless my obedience. And it is not always easy to give your total trust to God. In my own life, I've noticed that when I pray for something and it doesn't happen on my own time, I want to take it back from God and try to make it happen on my own. **Psalms 37:3** tells us to, "Trust in the Lord, and do good; Dwell in the land, and feed on His faithfulness" You may need some help on this one, completely trusting and allowing God to do His work.

When I had my own business, I did eventually quit my job, even though it brought in a great income. I earned a free car from my business and had a great team of women working with me who wanted more out of life. I abandoned the thought of failing. I abandoned the thoughts that I could not do this. I believed I could do it, and I expected a great return for it. I excelled in my business. Over time, though, my focus fell away and my business suffered because of that. It was all about doing what you needed to do to be successful, while understanding that what you put in would be what you got out of it.

One day, I got a phone call with a great, highly paid offer for a position in management. I told myself that I could do that and keep my business going. I did not make it happen. I took that job, and then I was focusing on two things, which is almost impossible to do without great discipline and determination. There were times I was on top of the world (when I had done the work), and there were times when I set goals and got a phone call at the last minute that helped me finish them. There were other times I sat back and doubted the whole thing, because I was starting to look at the circumstances. I would look at the people who let me down, not doing what they had said they would do.

I eventually let go of my leadership position with my business and from that day forward I was more focused on the job. I don't consider this a failure; it opened a lot of opportunities for me to minister and prove to myself that I could do whatever I set my mind to do. I expected great things to come, and I was confident I could do it. The choices I made determined my outcome and I know God was with me along the way.

REFLECTION POINTS

- Taking care of the elderly will bring many blessings
- God wants our obedience

Chapter 6
Ukraine and Belgium, An Answered Prayer

Have you ever prayed for something and felt like God didn't answer you? Have you ever decided that this *no answer* meant *a no* for you, so you tried to make your prayers come to life on your own?

A few weeks ago, I was sitting outside with a friend and we were talking about our kids and what was going on in their lives. I mentioned something about answered prayer and my friend said, "I don't know how I feel about God right now. I think I am just mad at Him. He hasn't answered a prayer of mine for over 20 years." It broke my heart, so I shared **Psalm 37** with her, "God wants to grant the desires of your heart" (NIV), and I told her a story about God answering one of my prayers much later in life.

To the Nations?

One of my prayers, many years ago, was that I could go on a mission trip to other nations to allow

God to use me to spread the Gospel. In **Matthew 28:19**, Jesus tells his disciples, "Therefore, go and make disciples of all the nations." I wanted to serve others and be a channel for God. I wanted to be able to minister to others in foreign countries and help others accept Jesus' love. This was not a prayer I continued to repeat and 'beg' God for. I just wanted to be used in a place where I could make a difference. The thought of working with people in a foreign country was intriguing to me, as I wanted to learn about cultures and beliefs and to serve others. Never did I think that, many years later, God would grant me the desires in my heart so that I would be able to go.

Divine Connections

When I was first learning to care for my mom, I connected with a new friend in my church, Callie Boyd. I needed to talk to someone who might have a similar situation with their aging parents and someone suggested I call Callie. God is funny; He already knew where this was going. I called Callie, we met up at Starbucks, and within just a few minutes we determined that we knew each other already through other acquaintances. Callie had gone to high school with my little brother, and the conversation was full of all kinds of surprises. She was able to help me with some deep questions I had about moving my mom in with Tommy and me and I had a lot more peace from that time forward.

World Missions

Callie and her husband, Randy, have a non-profit organization called Prepare International. It is "a world mission group dedicated to seeing the Kingdom of God come more fully in our generation and the generations to come!" They operate in over 23 nations and they travel to them to mentor, train, equip and pray for leaders and workers. They serve within their nations to disciple, church plant, and attend to building God's kingdom here on earth.

In 2017, Callie had an opportunity to invite someone to attend an upcoming trip. Because Randy was taking care of a health issue, Callie was going to travel alone and she did not know who she could take or even if someone could come. She prayed one morning before church and asked God to put someone on her heart that she could invite. Tommy and I were the first people she and Randy saw that morning in church, and something stirred her to invite me. Just to be clear, I was not the only one she invited, but God knew I would be the one going.

At first, Tommy was not comfortable with the trip because I would be traveling to a foreign country with a lot of terrorist activity. I knew I was going to go, though, because when I was journaling and reading my Bible, God guided me to Isaiah 6:8, where I read, "Also, I heard the voice of the Lord, saying, whom shall I send, and who will go for us. Then said I, send me." I asked God and He answered me, clearly. Soon after that, Tommy blessed my going.

Here We Go

We headed out for our 10-day journey on 11/8/17. We headed to Kalush, Ukraine for a few days, then flew to Brussels, rode the train to St. Truiden, and were driven to Beringen, all in Belgium. I wasn't worried about the possible dangers. Even when we landed at the airport in Brussels, there was damage and a lot of rebuilding going on due to a bomb that had gone off a few months before. The people there were quiet and they kept their heads down. Callie later told me that this was more cultural than anything. People did not talk to each other unless they were with a group. Women would be careful to not make eye contact with men, because in their country, men could receive this as an advance towards them. I kept my head down, but I never felt afraid for my safety. I also wasn't worried about what Callie had asked me to teach because I was too excited about how God was going to use me. When I look back, I think that maybe the peacefulness I was experiencing was God's way of protecting my mind from all the *what-ifs*.

After our long flight, we were welcomed at the airport by Pastor Vadim Kondratiuk, who took us to his church, where we would stay over the next few days. It was a very large and beautiful church. There was a small bedroom and bath in a back corner of the second floor, so we were tucked in a safe place. We were welcomed with fruit, snacks, pizza, and drinks. We had been traveling for hours and were so tired, however the meal was such a blessing, and we gratefully partook of it just before we went to bed.

Callie? Callie? What's That Noise?

We thought we were going to easily get to sleep, but we didn't—at least I didn't. I had had a little bit too much caffeine, so I was restless. As I lay there, I started hearing noises and thinking, *seriously?* I finally whispered loudly, "Callie? Callie?" and she woke up to my call. There was a crackling noise. It would go on and then it would stop. Then it would go again and then it would stop again. She told me, "Those are the radiator heaters on the wall," and I thought, *dang, okay. Sorry I woke you, girl.*

About 20 minutes later, I heard a *knock-knock-knock* at the door downstairs. I could not imagine who would be knocking. We were all alone in this large church, so who would be wanting in at this hour of the night. I heard it again, *knock knock knock*, but louder this time. I called out to my friend again, "Callie?

Callie? Someone is knocking on the door downstairs!" She rustled in her bed and sighed a little. Then she asked me, "What's wrong?"

I told her I heard knocking on the door downstairs. We lay listening for it again, until he finally knocked again, and this time was yelling. It was a man's voice. And not a language we understood. Callie got up and looked out the window from our room and there was a man across the parking lot trying to get in his own home. No one was letting him in the house and, with his yelling, it sounded like there may have been a little drinking involved. I apologized to Callie again.

The next night, something was flying around in our room. Not a little fly or mosquito either; it sounded very large. I swung at it with my hand as it circled my head, and I could tell it was very large when my hand touched it. I whispered to Callie to wake up. We were both up swinging things at something crossing the room in the air without knowing what it was, until one of us hit it. We looked around and could not find it. I hadn't anticipated that I would have so much difficulty getting to sleep away from my bed at home. In His faithfulness, though, God ensured I was still energized to teach the next morning.

The Teaching Begins

The next day, we started teaching in a large classroom there in the church and it was one of the most amazing times in my life. I just pinched myself to be sure it was truly happening. I had never worked with an interpreter and I didn't know any of the languages the students spoke, even though a few students did speak English. The teaching was centered around God's word, and we tied in our personal stories to help them make the connection better. I will never forget the testimonies that the students shared after our teaching and how our stories affected them. I journaled each day to help me stay connected to the emotions that I felt and what God did in my heart.

The people in Ukraine had such humble hearts, and they love the Lord so much. They are hungry for the Word, hungry to share, and hungry to serve. I remember so many of their faces, as we taught, and I wanted to bring them all home with me. The second day after training a young man came up to me with a pastor because he wanted to share an experience that he'd had through an interpreter. He told me that he always thought that American women had it made and had no problems. They dressed nicely, lived in nice houses, and drove fancy cars. After hearing my story about the loss of my son, he changed his perspective. He told me that he had walked through a lot of trials but held strong in his faith. His testimony blessed me so very much.

Me? Preach? What Are You Thinking?

Later that day, the pastor who was hosting us and a pastor there for training came up to Callie and me and asked if we would preach in their churches for Sunday service. I was shocked, then the fear kicked in. A voice in my head was saying, "Who do you think you are? You aren't a preacher; you are a teacher!" I just stood there waiting for Callie to answer, and of course she accepted. I hesitated and said, "I will pray about it."

Then, Callie, smiled and said, "Yes, she will preach," and as I said, "yes" I started going into panic mode. I was in a foreign country. I was going to have to ride over an hour away with a stranger, Svetlana, and no Callie. *What was I going to share about? What in the world was I doing?* Callie was very calm and told me to minister what was on my heart. I looked in my iPad at some messages I'd saved after sharing them with other groups in the past. I changed these messages to fit my situation and prayed that God would fill my mouth with His words.

Preaching, God Did It

When I went to preach, I had never been in a position where people just wanted to serve other people. Before the service, the pastor prayed over me, then we prayed together for a while. I brought a message to the people and some amazing things happened as God tugged on hearts. People were so open to hearing God's word. I taught about committing your ways to the Lord. I had them write on paper and bring forward the things they needed to let go of and place them in a trash can to signify letting go, not to take back. I brought their notes home with me and put them on poster board on a wall so I could continue praying over them.

Even though people there are very private, they poured their hearts out to God that day! They came forward at the end of the service for prayer time with me and we had a wonderful time in the Lord. So many of them let go of worry, issues with health, issues with dark thoughts, and family hurts, only to mention a few. They sincerely committed those things to God with new trust and hope. I thank God for allowing me to be His mouthpiece to share his love to the Nations.

REFLECTION POINTS

- God will always give you what you need in that moment you need it
- Commit your ways and concerns to God, letting go and not taking back

Belgium

The next day we flew to Brussels to spend a couple of days with Peter and Laura, a family involved with Prepare International. They have three children and lived in a small apartment downtown Brussels. Brussels is a beautiful rich city; however, it was a very different atmosphere from Texas. There are 170 nationalities living in that area. As we toured downtown, there was an army of men with machine guns who walked the square, ready for any threat. It was a little unnerving to me. Callie explained the difference in cultures to me. A lot of people in Brussels suffer with depression and, when they are depressed, they don't have to go to work if their doctor gives them a letter for their employer. They also believe in the Kevorkian Method of assisted suicide. It was a sobering yet revealing couple of days, and I knew that I wanted to learn more.

Can We Make a Difference?

One night, Callie taught to a group of ladies, and, again, you could see the hunger in their faces and the excitement they had as she spoke to them. I remember going back to the apartment that night and lying in bed, wide awake, asking God, "How can we make a difference for so many people who are hurting?" Then I was reminded of Billy Graham and how it takes only one person to impact the world. I rested after that with a good night's sleep.

During all this time I watched the hand of God in everything. I prayed as we walked. I prayed when we visited the churches on the square. I wasn't sure of some of the cultural differences, but I prayed the entire time that God would show me what I needed to know and that He would protect me from the things I did not need to know. I just wanted to soak in everything I could. Every night, I journaled so that I didn't forget a thing. God was by our side all the while, and we knew it.

REFLECTION POINT

- If we can help JUST ONE person, it could change the world.

On To St. Truiden

We ventured the next day to St. Truiden, Belgium to stay with a friend, Madelaine. We didn't have anything on the agenda other than to spend time with her. She and her husband, Conley (now living in Heaven) have been a part of Prepare International for a long while and pastored a church there in St. Truiden. It was good for us to be there with just the three of us, as her husband was on a mission trip. Madelaine took us around town, we drank black tea, ate pancakes, shopped a bit, and talked until we couldn't talk any more (no interpreter needed). Once again, we were treated like royalty. I kept thanking God for all that was happening. He had us there for a reason. Now, Madelaine carries on the work she and Conley had started.

REFLECTION POINT

- You may not know why God has you in a specific place at a specific time but being obedient will bring blessings.

On To Beringen

The next day, we traveled on to Beringen to stay with pastors Willie and Esther Smit. Callie forewarned me that Willie was typically a man of few, yet important words. However, on this trip he was enjoyably talkative. We were welcomed into their home. They treated us like royalty again. Esther was such a great hostess, making sure we were comfortable, fed and rested up. Their children were so respectful and serving other people was part of who they were. That Saturday, we taught God's word through a series of lessons with a wonderful group of eager participants. I shared parts of my story throughout. We had one man there who was previously with the Mafia, and his story (that he shared through an interpreter) brought me to tears. His love for Christ now has such a depth to it and he wants others to know the same.

Callie taught and was fully anointed with her message. It was a draining day, and we were tired, however, refreshed from pouring into these wonderful people. The next day was Sunday and Callie was going to preach at Pastor Willie's church. I remember going to bed thinking, *Whew! Tomorrow I can relax and listen to Callie. I am safe from speaking!*

Not so fast, though. The next morning, just before we left the breakfast table, Pastor Willie asked me to share my testimony at the start of service. I got flutters in my stomach, and then said, "Yes, of course I will speak," because, by that point, Callie had taught me well. Again, God was teaching me about obedience and just GOing!

When we got to the church and saw the people, I knew there would be someone there that my story would speak to in a way that glorified God. At the end of the service, we held special ministry so that people could come to the front and we prayed for them. It was amazing. Pastor Willie shared his heart for Pakistan and some stories about ministering to people there in spite of dangerous conditions. The church was so committed to the Lord's mission for them that they weren't even afraid of the dangers. They knew they were protected.

REFLECTION POINT

- Always be ready to share your story, Say YES!

My Mission Trip—My Message

I started out this section referring to God answering prayers and my mission trip was a turning point for me in trusting God for answers. Please know this: If God can use me, He can use anyone. Don't be afraid to put your desires out there to God. Pray for them, even if they seem unreachable. God tells us in **Psalm 37** that He wants to grant the desires of our heart. Ask yourself, "What am I wanting from the Lord?" and then I encourage you to seek Him for it and trust that it will happen according to His perfect timing and perfect order.

The Rest of the Story

Remember the story from my second night in Belgium about something flying in our room in the dark? I was unpacking when we got back home in the States. After I emptied my backpack, I turned it upside down and a large, dead bumblebee fell out of my bag. It was a beautiful dead bee, colors still sharp, wings perfect, all still intact, and I use it today to share my testimony. For me, it reminded me of how we can look good on the outside but—on the inside—we are spiritually dead. For Callie, the bee reminded her of how the lives that we carry zap out all the bad stuff! Either way it is an amazing reminder of God's goodness.

REFLECTION POINTS

- Just GO! When you know you are being called by God; Expect the good stuff when you are being pushed out of your comfort zone
- God always makes provision for us
- Even a dead bumble bee can represent God's goodness

Chapter 7
My 2020

Who knew that, two years after I returned from the Ukraine and Belgium, my future would be full of new challenges? God continued to add to my story.

On 12/29/19, I wrote in my journal, "Renewing my mind with God's word is one of the most important things I can do. I must think in an entirely new way. Transformed means to be changed completely. According to a new inner reality, change me God from the inside out! Help me see things from your perspective. Give me a fresh desire to read—study and apply your word in every single area of my life. In Jesus name I pray—Amen. For 2020 I will see:

BREAKTHROUGH, SELF-CARE, MIRACLES, FAMILY AND PURPOSE."

Little did I know that, when I wrote the things I envisioned for my life in 2020, my year would include miracles and self-care with health, family, breakthroughs, and a stronger sense of passion and purpose. My story continues.

I'll Never Forget This Day

January 31, 2020. Have you ever had one of those days where you were on top of the world, and you were in your element doing what you loved to do, working with your special gifts that give you joy, when *POW!* The brakes went on and you were done. January 31, 2020 was one of those days for me. I was working for Keller Williams Realty as Director of W.O.W. where I **W**elcomed and **O**nboarded new agents, then **W**alked with *all* of our agents. I worked with a team of leaders who had your back, who poured into your work every single day, who stretched you to be your best self, and who always taught to not give up but to *solve for yes* (a solution). We are a family and, even though I no longer work there as an employee, I am there in spirit and I post on our social media daily to encourage our agents and celebrate them.

This day was filled with appointments to enroll new agents at our office. We had welcome appointments in which I signed people up who were joining from other offices, and our monthly Ignite session with new agents. It was a packed day, and an exciting one! I had been on cloud nine most of the day when I noticed that I had a scratchy, little cough. I also had some swelling in my legs, ankles, and face, but it wasn't too noticeable. Just enough to bother me. I had also noticed in the past few weeks that, periodically, when I went to the bathroom my urine was discolored a bit. The discoloration always went away, though, so I did not give it much thought. I felt good, I had been to my annual checkup in December, and everything was perfect.

At 3:30 that afternoon, though, I hit a wall. I just could not go on. I had to leave right away and go home. I had no energy, my cough was getting worse, and I suddenly felt like I had been hit by a truck. I left without even telling my boss, as she was leading the training session for new agents. It was their graduation day, and I had been so excited to participate in that event, but not anymore.

Over the next three days I was in two different doctor's offices and both doctors thought my symptoms were minor. They expressed no concern over swelling and my little cough, so I finally told my primary care doctor, "Something is wrong! I don't get sick!" She agreed to do some blood work and said she would call me as soon as she got it. I expected to get that call the same day and that did not happen. In the meantime, I was in bed, very sick.

Emergency Room, Now!

The next morning, she called early and told me to go immediately to the ER; I had no kidney function at all. Tommy quickly drove me to the ER where everything started to spin out of control. I had nurses, doctors, and other staff checking in on me. I had needles in me, testing going on, questions, and more questions. I just couldn't understand what was going to happen and certainly did not understand how sick I was.

My doctor came in and started asking more questions. They were going to admit me and run more tests. In the meantime, a couple of my co-workers came into the ER with me and brought me a Starbucks. I could not drink anything because I had no kidney function and I had to tell them I couldn't have it. There was no urine going out, everything was building up in my body, hence the swelling. Toxins were on the rise and they had to do something fast. I got wheeled off to a room after a few hours in the ER and that was the beginning of more bad news and an 11-day stay in the hospital.

The entire time, I was worried. I was scared. I couldn't understand what was happening to me, and it suddenly became a very dark time in my life. Have you ever been in this position of not knowing whether to be worried, or to just let the doctors do their job? Have you ever encountered a fear of the unknown?

What Next?

God was with me all that time and I knew that, but I did not exactly feel his presence. I felt more like I was sinking into a dark hole. After one day, my doctor decided to go ahead and do a kidney biopsy to determine what had caused this shutdown. Those tests can take three to four days for results. I was wheeled downstairs to have the biopsy and, when I got back upstairs, I had a catheter in my neck with all these little tubes coming out of it. I was told I was going to dialysis. *Talk about scary!* "If I go on dialysis," I thought, "I can never come off. What in the world is happening? Four days ago, I was just fine!" But I just followed the doctor's orders and avoided drinking more than 32 oz of fluid daily, which was regulated very carefully.

After the third day, I was going in and out of darkness in my mind. I was scared and confused, but I knew I had to get my head right. I had been on morphine for the pain from the new catheter, but I woke up at 4 AM the next morning and I heard God whisper, "Quit fighting, I will fight for you. You just rest." I remember taking a deep breath and letting out a sigh. The message from God helped me relax and gave me some much-needed peace.

My Quiet Time

The next day, a window opened for some quiet time, so I got out my journal and started writing. I needed to change my focus. I had been focused on the circumstances and they were not good, and now I was afraid of what the outcome might be. I started writing down all the circumstances of what was going on. It looked like this:

CIRCUMSTANCES: SICK—SUDDENLY—DOCTORS DIDN'T LISTEN TO ME—UNCERTAIN—RARE DISEASE—WHY ME?—DIALYSIS?—FOREVER?—SCARED; FIGHTING FOR MY LIFE; URGENT CARE; IGNORED SYMPTOMS; FEEL AWFUL; WHAT IS HAPPENING. BIOPSY; CATHETER; DIALYSIS; ULTRASOUND; BLACK HOLE; CAN'T PEE

Then at the top of my page, I wrote—'WHAT I KNOW'. It looked like this:

- **Mark 11:23**—I speak to the mountain with great faith—no doubting—it will be done.
- **Eph 6:11**—Put on God's complete set of armor provided for me, so I am protected as I fight against the evil strategies of the devil. Jesus is the lord of my life, sickness and disease have no power over me.
- Jesus bore my sickness and carries my pain. By his stripes, I am healed. I give no place to sickness or pain. God sent his word and healed me.
- **Ps 107:20**—I have abundant life and I receive it through every organ of my body—bringing healing and health.

- **John 10:10, John 6:63**—My God is with me. I will focus on these things, not on the circumstances.

I wrote down blessings, including the people who had been involved thus far in getting me to where I was now: Tommy, Scott, Chelsea, Kathy, Lee, Tara, LeighAnn, Jason, Julie, Evanna, Tim, Donna, Paige, Linda, my Keller Williams family, my immediate family. There was so much support and there were so many prayers. My doctor's decision to start dialysis instead of waiting three days for a test result had saved my life. He did not wait; he knew we couldn't.

Coincidently (or not, *wink*), two weeks prior to this mess, I had interviewed my doctor's wife, Nishma, to come to Keller Williams as a new agent. I immediately fell in love with her, and we were instant friends. That divine connection was a blessing and I am confident that God was in control of that. I will be forever grateful my doctor moved so fast to get answers.

Momma, No!

Two days later, my mother, 90 years old, fell and broke her hip at the nursing home close by. They brought her to the same hospital I was in and, as God would give us favor, she was two floors directly below me. I was able to go visit her before her surgery. It was heartbreaking to see her this way, knocked out with pain medication and still moaning.

There was so much going on! My sisters, brother, and niece came to be with her. She had to have hip surgery and spend a couple of days in hospital before they moved her back to the nursing home. She had been so worried about me because I visited her almost daily at the nursing home. When I got sick, the visits stopped suddenly, and with her progressive dementia, she did not understand why I hadn't been to visit her. I don't know if she ever really understood what had happened to me, but I think that she knew it was not good.

My Diagnosis

The next day my doctors determined my diagnosis. I had a very rare disease, nicknamed Goodpasture's Syndrome. One in 1.6 million people are affected with this disease. I remember hearing these words from the doctor, and I immediately thought, "Lord, I knew I was special and set apart, but really? For this?" All kinds of things were going through my mind. This auto-immune disorder is a disease that causes antibodies to attack the lungs and kidneys. Long-term survival is over 50%. It can be fatal if not quickly diagnosed and treated. My doctor had saved my life with his quick decisions.

My doctor had told me to not become Dr. Google. It was better to stay off the internet to get information. He did not want me to worry, he just wanted me to let him take care of me. I did not become Dr. Google, but my family did because they were very concerned. I have two nephews who are doctors, and they were full of concern; the disease sounds very scary and serious when you read about it.

I stayed in the hospital for eight more days, doing dialysis and blood tests daily. My arms and wrists were so bruised from all the needles and tubes they had put in me. After dialysis, I would come back to my room so exhausted that I wanted to cry. I knew I had to be strong and focus on what God says about me in His word, rather than on circumstances.

Going Home

I was sent home after eleven days and was doing dialysis three times a week for four hours at a time. I dreaded going to the dialysis center. Watching machines take blood out and put blood back in people might be interesting to some people, but I personally hated it. I hated how it made me feel. A lot of people on dialysis are very sick, and it was a very sad place to come to and sit for four hours. When COVID kicked into high gear, I felt very concerned because my immune system was a mess.

Right away, I decided I had to have some spiritual ammunition with me in the form of my Bible, journal, colored pencils, a scripture book to color, my iPad so I could listen to music, and books to read. I always carried in my bag loaded with things that gave me joy. I can count on one hand how many people I saw do the same. In fact, right now I can only remember two other people who were doing something constructive with this passing time. It made me very thankful I had learned mindset skills over the years past that helped me not to give into the negative. I knew I had a choice to solve for a solution. And it was going to be a good one. When we live too much in our head, it can be a scary thing!

Now, a Heart Attack??

April came around and I was headed to a doctor's appointment when my husband, Tommy, told me to wait up. He was not feeling well and he needed to go to the ER. His chest and left arm were hurting badly, and he was concerned. I waited a few minutes and when he said, "Let's go!" I knew it was serious. He does not like to go to doctors. He was having a heart attack. Tommy had been taking such good care of me, that he neglected taking care of himself. I could not go in with him to the ER because I was immunocompromised, and I could not risk contracting COVID. I called Scott, my son in Midland, and he came right away. Tommy had to have surgery the next morning, to correct the blockage in his veins with two stints. I hated not being there, but I was at peace because Scott was with him and God, as He'd always done, took care of Tommy. Soon, we were both at home, in quarantine, immunocompromised, and waiting to get better.

Kidney Transplant?

One afternoon, while I was in dialysis, my doctor stopped by and told me that the chemo drugs that they'd been giving me to jump start my kidneys were not working as they had hoped. I needed to get on a transplant list. "Here we go again," I thought, "How in the world does that work?" I went through the detailed steps to get on the list. They did more tests, had phone calls, had interviews with doctors in Dallas, and a lot of screenings of my emotions. I did feel emotional, too. "Who in the world will give me a kidney?" I would think, "Some people wait for years to get a kidney." I had seen little children on dialysis and cried for them; it broke my heart, and now I needed a transplant.

My doctor also suggested I start doing my dialysis at home, and that scared me. Tommy and I were certainly not trained to do everything that had to be done, but Dr. Patel and his staff trained us. I was plugged into that machine for ten hours at night and I had to do manual treatments four hours during the day. It was a constant drain on me. I went into counseling over the phone and I cried and felt sorry for myself. I tried to do my best by focusing on God, but I had too much going on. I just wanted to go to sleep and then wake up all healed and normal again.

In this position, I certainly grew more compassionate for others who could not even get on a transplant list. For some people on dialysis, their health would not allow them to be a candidate. I wondered how they did it, thinking, *How do they keep existing like this?* It was heart-breaking and I was constantly reminded of my sister, Beth, who had Multiple Sclerosis and died of complications from Leukemia. She had been in bed for over 30 years and was unable to have any independence. *How did she do that?* "Oh, Lord," I prayed, "Help me appreciate that I have some options here, and please keep me strong until we get this figured out!"

Chelsea First

We passed the news to my kids that I needed a kidney transplant. Chelsea and Scott were the first to come forward offering to give me a kidney. Due to his recent heart attack and surgery for stints, Tommy was not strong enough to be accepted as a candidate. Chelsea immediately began researching what to do, but when she got tested, she was not a match. She could do paired matching, though, where she exchanged her kidney for another person's kidney if the other person's kidney was a match for me. She was ready to do it if we didn't have other options. Scott wanted to try next, and I also had other family members and friends with my blood type who wanted to help—a friend in South Dakota, my niece, Tracy, and even my dental hygienist wanted to try. It gave me such peace to know that God was working this out.

Scott Next

Scott started doing his testing. I worried because I didn't want either of my kids to be in pain or to take that chance on the operating table. There was always a risk, but a little whisper told me, "It's okay. It's covered." Scott had to do repeat blood work a couple of times that sometimes had to be sent to the CDC for review testing. He went to Dallas and sat with a team of doctors and psychologists who interviewed him for an entire day to be sure he was emotionally stable and to express to them why he was doing this. I was so happy he wanted to help me, but I had reservations at the same time. *What if he needed his kidney for someone else later???* The testing turned up one thing after another. They never told us no, but we were delayed for at least two months before we got a yes; he was a match!

By this time, it was late September, and we were eight months into this ordeal. Scott called me one morning and I tried to have a casual conversation with him, but I was anxious to find out if he was a match and we were clear for surgery. Finally, I asked him, "Did you hear anything from anyone yet?" And he nonchalantly said, "Oh yeah. We are good to go." *What? What did you say? Did you say that? We are cleared to go? You are a match??* The tears started to flow. I was so happy. I was so tired from the last eight months and I wanted my life to go back to normal; I just wanted to be healthy again. Scott told me we had a surgery date for November 2nd, 2020. That was music to my ears! I thanked God repeatedly for His faithfulness.

Blessed by Support

The same day Scott got approved, my Keller William's family called me and said they had decided to do a fundraiser at an annual event they were all attending. Everyone was so generous and I was speechless when they explained to me how much they had raised. My niece, Tracy, also started a GoFundMe account to support us. Even my sister's friend, Jan, who did not know me well made a generous donation. Richard and Ginger Davila were selfless in their support, and so many more. Because we would be in Dallas for three to six weeks before we could come back home, Tommy, our kids, and I would have numerous expenses. At first, we felt pride and thought, "We don't need that," but God knew we did and He continued to make provision for our needs. We could never thank those enough for how they supported us in that way.

Why Delays?

I want to talk about delays. I love that our God always has the right timing and the right order for everything. During my illness, I had become impatient, frustrated, and mad at times. I wanted the transplant to happen now, because I was tired of all the tubes, the machines, and safety measures we had to take care of daily. God reminded me of **Mark 4:26-28**, "And He said, the kingdom of God is like a man who scatters seed upon the ground. And then continues sleeping and rising night and day while the seed sprouts and grows and 'increases—he knows not how. The earth produces by itself—first the blade, then the ear, then the full grain in the ear. Simply, the farmer sows his seed in the ground and then goes about his other business. The ground will bring forth a yield in due season. He leaves the rest in God's hands"

I was reminded that delays are not denials and I started wondering *why* we were being delayed. Maybe a particular nurse or a doctor needed to take care of me or Scott. Maybe there was something we were going to be able to do to bless someone during that hospital stay. These passing thoughts kept me in peace about the delay.

The Transplant

When I went to bed the night before the surgery, I was still on the dialysis machine for 10 hours at night. I remember thanking God over and over that it was the last time I had to be dependent on that machine to keep me alive. It was humbling and made me so grateful for technology and the things that are available to sustain life. Who would have ever thought that I would need something like that at 65 years old!

We had the surgery November 2, 2020, two days after my 65th birthday. The fact that I had not been able to pee in 10 months is difficult for me to grasp now, but once they got that kidney of Scott's transplanted into me, the magic started on the operating table. They told me the story and it was kind of funny. When I woke from surgery, I had a bag at the end of the bed with a catheter and I was filling that bag up every little bit! I couldn't believe it! They completely changed my diet from what it was and said that *Yes! I could have a diet coke. Yes! I could eat things high in potassium.* I was so excited to drink coke. It had been ten months since I had had anything other than water.

Going Home

Scott did amazingly well after surgery. He was very sore and did not walk until the next day. I felt so bad about him hurting. I got out of bed before he did because I wanted to see him so bad. We were just across the hall from each other. Our first contact after surgery was teary. I was so grateful, and at the same time, sorry he was in pain.

We did all the things they told us to do to have a successful recovery. Those first 10 days were truly hard. There was a lot of pain and discomfort with any movement. We were staying in an apartment together and we went for walks every little while. We rested a lot. Scott went home the next week and I had to stay another week. Blood work is crucial after you get a new kidney to be sure you aren't going to reject it. Medication is equally as crucial to the recovery. I had to learn a lot.

Because of God's faithfulness, we both have done extremely well. I get checked monthly now to be sure my kidney is still working, and Scott gets his kidney checked periodically. It is amazing what can be done with a surgery like that. I came out of there with a whole new outlook on life. I know we both did.

So Much I Learned

In closing this chapter, I know that I experienced a lot of adversity, waiting, delays in treatment, fear, confusion, pain, and darkness, but I want to express to you this fact: I never felt ALONE. Yes, I was in a dark place, and I didn't understand what was going on, but I knew God's word was true and I knew his promises were yes and amen. I knew **Isaiah 41:10** and it was a rock for me, "Fear not, for I am with you. Be not dismayed, for I am your God. I will strengthen you, yes I will help you, I will uphold you with my righteous right hand." These days, I share this scripture a lot with friends who are going through a scary or dark time or who just don't feel like they are on solid ground. God is always there, holding you by His right hand. What a wonderful promise from our father! In times of darkness and fear, seek a place of peace, ask God for peace, then take these messages and ask God what He is saying to you.

HAPPY NOTE: Remember how I talked about delays not being denials and how I started wondering if my surgery was being delayed because a doctor or nurse needed something while I was there? One afternoon, one of my nurses came into my room, and I felt led to give her a little encouragement card with scripture and two messages in it. I carry these with me everywhere I go and I asked permission to give her the card. She was so pleased. She cried a little and said the message I'd given her was so perfect. She came back to my room later and asked me to sign her card; she said it made her day. We don't know what other people are going through, so please keep your hearts and eyes open to be aware to speak encouragement to others when you feel led.

REFLECTION POINTS

- You are never alone
- Delays aren't denials
- Focus on His promises, not the circumstances

Chapter 8
Peace Plan

As I transition to this new chapter, I want to share with you how-to live-in peace, even though things are going awry in your life. When I talked to Pastor Paige Allen about needing to express all the things God has taught me, she asked me how in the world I could have gotten through all the trials, because these trials were not little things, they were big things.

I had to think about it for a moment, when God reminded me of a message He had shared with me many years ago through a friend, Dean Eldridge, in Dallas, Texas. Dean had shared this message one Sunday in church, and I could not write notes fast enough. The message was about having a Plan for Peace, regardless of what was going on in your life. This message is one I have carried with me and have shared with numerous people. God has used it in several different scenarios. I was able to teach it in the Ukraine and Belgium on my mission trip. I have shared it at several women's conferences in Oklahoma and Texas, and it has been life changing.

Draw Your Circle

There are four different parts to the message, and I encourage you to do what Dean suggests: Draw a circle and divide it into four separate sections, one line down the middle and one line across the middle.

The sections are as follows:
- Top Left—COMMIT
- Top Right—TRUST
- Bottom Right—DELIGHT
- Bottom Left—REST

I will share with you how you can apply this in your life, daily and how it has helped me to get through many difficult experiences. Take some notes, draw the circle, make it personal so that you can integrate it into your life. Dean's teaching is taken from the Psalms.

Section 1: COMMIT

Psalm 37:5 says, *"Give God the right to direct your life, and as you trust him along the way, you'll find he pulled it off perfectly"* *(TPT).*

I love this translation from the Passion Bible. Early in the morning, I start my day by committing it to Him. This means your *whole day*. That means *everything in your day!* That way, you can rest assured that whatever happens during that day was all designed by Him. He took your commitment, and He took it seriously, as His word does not return void. He wants to take care of those things to which you commit. You can commit your words, your steps, your actions, and anything else on your heart. Once committed, you can roll off the load, because He knows what is ahead! Pray a prayer of relinquishment—truly surrender what you committed. Once committed, you can't take it back. And that is where it can get tough. Sometimes we want things to happen more quickly than God is working, and we want to take matters into our own hands. However, performing an act to show your commitment helps you to remember it later.

At one of the women's conferences, I had them write down the things they were committing to God, and we took it outside and set it on fire. We burned it, as an act of commitment. To let go of all the negative junk is so freeing. Once it was burned, no one could get it back. I have had other groups bury it in the ground after writing down. They couldn't dig it up. When I was in the Ukraine, I had them bring their commitments forward and put them in a trash can up front. No names, just what they had committed. I brought them back to America, so they could not physically take them back.

If you don't know how to really commit, ask God to show you how. Then FORGET IT. He will honor our requests when we commit to Him. (**II Tim 1:12. Ps 35:5-6; Jer 33:3; Acts 20:32**). Test God's word, it does not return void. He promises us that.

Corporate Favor

At one time, I was working for an American multinational financial services company/bank. They are in 35 countries and many of you probably bank there. They have 70 million customers. I am one of them! I don't mention the Corporate Name to protect anyone that could get reprimanded for allowing what I am about to share with you. I tell you this story so you can get a glimpse of how big our God is!

I was a Lending Officer and, with the help of one other person, I monitored production and quality for 145 underwriters. One day, soon after I had started working in the position, one of the employees came to me and asked me if I was a Christian. I told her I was and she asked me to be in a prayer group that they wanted to start. I didn't even hesitate, thinking it would be three or four people. The first day, we met in a closet, closed the door, and prayed, holding hands. There were four people. The next day, we had to go into a small copy room with six to seven people. Within a week, we had to take over a very large room and, I can only guess, but there were probably thirty or more people in that room, holding hands, praying for each other. We prayed for our communities, our jobs, health, families, and anything else that came up. I was participating, but not leading as I was in a management position and could not be partial to our employees. I was a bit nervous when we grew so fast, and for good reason. I had already committed this prayer group to God. I knew God wanted our time with Him in His presence; I was just not sure how we would be able to continue.

The next week, I got a phone call from someone in upper management who asked if I was leading a prayer group. She had seen us praying when she got to work. We started early but, as the group grew, we were getting to our desks a little after 8 AM. I told her I was participating, and she said the head boss would want to meet with me when he got back into town. Before our meeting, I prayed so much for God's favor and I committed our prayer group to Him, as he tells us to. I trusted He would do what was best for us and I felt at peace after I truly committed this to him.

Meeting with the BIG BOSS

I got the call and met with the BIG BOSS and his first words were, "Are you leading a prayer group?" I told him that I was participating. He confirmed that was the position I needed to be in, not leading, since I was a leader in the company, working with management. He then thanked me for having community with those who desired to be better and to have a closer walk with God. He wanted us to continue meeting, but with some boundaries, that were reasonable. We had to meet early, and still arrive on time to work or to meet over lunch. He also gave us our own room to meet and pray in. This was truly a miracle. Not only did God meet us with favor to continue the group, but we even got a room to pray in! Commit it all to him and watch what happens.

Section 2: TRUST

Psalm 37:3 says, "Trust in the Lord and do good: dwell in the land and enjoy safe pasture" (NIV).

Once you have truly committed, you now get to trust God to do what He says He will do. What is trust, though? It is the confident expectation of something, of hope. You can't make a place for doubt in your life and you can't expect the blessing without completely trusting God. You must have faith. **James 2:8** says, "Faith without action is dead." You must believe in His faithfulness. This is where you go to work.

Before my healing from Multiple Sclerosis, I had to totally commit healing to God and then trust that He had the best life for me. I chose to walk it out in faith. When Blake died, I asked God to allow me to meet Jeremy Camp so that I could talk to him about the song playing in Blake's CD player before he got in his plane for the last time. I asked God, then trusted Him to deliver. And He did. That came about in a miraculous way.

Lev 26:9 says, "God will be leaning toward you with favor!" **Rom 15:13** says, "To bubble over with Hope, I abound in Hope." Has anyone ever told you to not get your hopes up? I was talking to my son, Scott, one afternoon about a job interview he had for a job that he really wanted. He told me that everything went well, but he was not going to get his hopes up. I responded, "Who's kid are you?? You get your hopes up! Yes, sir!" God wants us to get our hopes up for the things we are trusting Him for, so I might ask you, what are you trusting God for right now? What have you asked Him for that you're not confident about? If you're not confident, you are trying to take matters back into your own hands because He hasn't answered that prayer the way that you wanted. Please internalize this message, these scriptures, and these promises, and then let it go with trust and faith. Watch Him work!

Section 3: DELIGHT

Psalm 37:4 says, *"Take delight in the Lord, and he will give you the desires of your heart."* NIV

We need to get excited about what God is doing in our lives. Because you've committed, be determined as you move towards the desires of your heart. He wants to give you an abundance of peace, so don't build resistance to good things coming your way. Sometimes, I think we may feel selfish asking God for *things*. We may think we don't deserve them. Instead, we settle. When we want what God wants—and when we want it for the same reason that God wants it for us—we will get it! God is *into* you paying your bills! God wants you healthy! God wants you to understand that His love is unconditional!

I have messed up a lot of things in my life, especially before I knew God's desire to have a personal relationship with me. I got a divorce at an early age to seek greener grass on the other side. I had two little boys and I was focused on *stuff* to make me happy. But God always stayed faithful to me, showing me His unconditional love. I prayed for my boys, wanting them to stay emotionally and physically healthy, and God granted that desire. My boys had their teenage moments, but God was always faithful. I know God was faithful because of the prayers I prayed when they were little, before I was even connected with God's truth.

Section 4: REST

Psalm 37:7 *says, "Be still before the Lord and wait patiently for him; do not fret when people succeed in their ways, when they carry out their wicked schemes" (NIV).*

God wants time with us. He wants us to be still, and to soak in his presence. He wants us to patiently wait for him. He wants us to rest. Sometimes, we can't do that in our own strength, and we must depend on His strength. If we don't rest, we are showing we don't have faith that God will provide us with time to do everything that we need to do. By giving our last word at night and our first word in the morning to the Lord, we can build our patience for this.

When I was in the hospital with my kidney failure, I was restless, I was scared, and I was confused. When God told me to quit fighting–that He would fight for me—He was asking me to rest. And it was clear when I heard His voice telling me to Rest. I can't say that was easy at first, but after all the hours of all those emotions, I finally realized I needed to *let go and let God*. From then on, I was able to rest better and to wait patiently for him to heal me. He says in His word to wait patiently. Infinite patience means that we have indefinite, unlimited patience. Can you even imagine having that kind of patience? I know God has that kind of patience with us. And I am forever grateful for it.

Fretting?
Out of the Plan

In **Ps 37:1**, the Word tells us to not FRET. The meaning of FRETTING is expressing worry, discontentment, or annoyance. God showed me how fretting causes us to get out of the PEACE PLAN. He showed me an acronym for FRET to explain it.

Forgot you committed.
Resisting good things coming our way.
Emotions—don't operate here.
Tired, will wear you out.

To keep it simple, when we begin fretting again with worry or discontentment, we **F**orget that we have committed to God. At this point, we must commit to God again. We must commit again and get into a habit of committing. We **R**esist good things coming our way when we forget that we committed and begin fretting. We operate out of **E**motion because we forgot that we have committed, and this emotion makes us **T**ired and worn out.

Do you have a peace plan? I encourage you to impart this message into your heart. Tuck it away. When you need it or when God reminds you of it, you can call on it and use it for your life to keep you in a place of peace.

REFLECTION POINTS

- Don't forget you committed
- Trust God to do the work you can't
- Fretting takes you out of the Peace Plan

Chapter 9
Declaration—What God Says!

As we come to the end of our time together, I am trusting God that you have gained some new insight from the things I have shared, and they can help you as your walk on your path. I want to close with a declaration message to give you some promises and thoughts about what God says about you and the fact that you can overcome anything in your path with Him as your rock and foundation. This is probably one of the most exciting things I can share with you, because, if you take it to heart and study what this message can mean for you, it can be a trajectory moment in your life that benefits you in your Calling.

One morning, in May 2015, I saw a post on Facebook by Pastor Kimberly Pothier Jones, that included a powerful Declaration. I wrote it in my journal and started downloading some parts of her message into my heart. It reminded me again of who I am and 'whose' I am. To those of you reading this book, may this Declaration touch you in a way that is special to you. May my story touch your life in a way that will help you to see that you can overcome whatever may come against you and that you can use it for good. You have a story to tell. We all have a story to tell. This is mine.

DECLARATION

- You are a Person of **DESTINY**.
- You are **EQUIPPED, CREATIVE** and You are Designed for a **PURPOSE**.
- You are **LOVED, CHOSEN,** and **ACCEPTED** BY Almighty God.
- There is **NOTHING YOU CAN DO TO MAKE GOD LOVE YOU MORE.**
- There is **NOTHING YOU CAN DO TO MAKE GOD LOVE YOU LESS.**
- His **GRACE** is **SUFFICIENT** for You.
- His **ANGELS** have Charge **OVER** You.
- You are **BLESSED COMING IN** and You are **BLESSED GOING OUT**.
- You have **UNCOMMON WISDOM, UNCOMMON JOY** and **UNCOMMON PEACE**.
- **GOD IS YOUR VINDICATOR.** He Will **FIGHT FOR YOU**.
- **NO WEAPON** Formed **AGAINST YOU WILL PROSPER AS YOU SERVE GOD** All the Days of Your Life. **AMEN!**

I want to break down some of these incredible words for you and share how they can become a part of your everyday walk.

DESTINY

Destiny: *predetermined, certainty, designed, expectation, ordinance, what is written, intent (**Jer 29:11; Luke 5:4**)*

I love God's word and how **Jeremiah 29:11** puts it on the line. "For I know the thoughts that I think toward you, says the Lord, thoughts of peace and not of evil, to give you a future and a hope." **Jeremiah 1:5** says, "Before I formed you in the womb, I knew you; Before you were born, I sanctified you, I ordained you a prophet to the nations." If we could just stop here and take these two scriptures and download them into our hearts and heads and repeat them over and over until we really believed it, then we would be contented to know that we know, that we know that God's plan for us is *good*!

In Chapter 1, I shared how my walk with the Lord did not actually begin to flourish until I was in my late 30s. I did not understand my purpose, I was learning on the way. God is faithful, and my destiny— just like your destiny—is a journey we get to take. It will be a roller coaster ride! It will get bumpy, it will hurt, and it will be great! It will be surprising; it will be predictable at times, but we get the choice to take the ride and make it a good one. We can only do that by focusing and holding on to what we *know* and not on what we *don't know*. God's word never changes, even if everything else does. He predetermined a life for you. He has a purpose for you. It is all good! Step out and find out! Don't be status quo! Take fear out of the equation. He did not give us a spirit of fear! But of power and love and of a sound mind (**2 Tim 1:7**).

In her Everyday Study Bible, Joyce Meyer talks about 'stepping out and finding out' and I love some of the things she says. She writes, "The only way we will ever fulfill our destinies and succeed at being our true selves is to take many steps of faith. Stepping out into the unknown and launching out into the deep water can be frightening." When I left my first marriage, I had two little boys, I did not have a job, but I was determined and stubborn enough to move out of our home. I was ignorant of God's word and I did not know what I was doing, but God's grace was sufficient. I felt bad for my boys—two years and four years old at the time—and I hated when they were unhappy and cried for their dad. But I kept moving forward.

Did I know this was part of my Destiny? NO, I did not, and I was not particularly enjoying it at the time either. Do I believe this was God's plan? I believe God gives us free will and it was a choice that I made. Looking back, I would not change it. Many things have happened to get me where I am today and, if I had stayed in that marriage, I would not be writing this story right now to help someone else.

Joyce Meyer also says, "Because of feelings of fear, many people never 'step out,' therefore they never find out what they are capable of. Each of us needs to obey God when He wants us to step out into something new or challenging. We are living in the dispensation of grace and many doors of opportunity are open to share the Gospel of Jesus Christ with others. Decide that you will not miss any opportunity that God gives you. Do what God asks you to do even if you must 'do it afraid.' Feel the fear and do it anyway."

When I think of my destiny being predetermined and designed with certainty, it boggles my mind. It goes back to a message from Beth Moore regarding how God thinks about us. He knew us before we were formed in our mother's womb, so he was thinking of me regardless of the decision I made based on emotion and ignorance.

My life story is still in the making. I am excited for all the things the Lord has taught me and continues to teach me. I am in a totally different time in my life now. My kids are all grown with one in Heaven, and I have grandkids to love on. I am unemployed due to health reasons, and Tommy and I are about to retire. We will never really retire, however, because we will still have choices to do things differently, and to do things with purpose.

EQUIPPED

Equip: *to provide whatever is needed; to prepare, appoint, assemble.*

Jeremiah 1:9 tells me that God put forth his hand and touched my mouth and said, "Behold, I have put my words in your mouth." Any time I am speaking to a group or to an individual, it is so important that I pray this scripture. I want to speak only God's words. When I started thinking about the word *equipped*, I thought back to several occasions where God has equipped both me and others. Equip means 'to have whatever is needed.'

I am sure that when the Israelites prepared to cross the Red Sea, they did not feel equipped with enough faith to do so, but once they stepped in, they walked ahead without turning back. They did not have time to figure it out. They were about to be killed by an army chasing them down. They had no choice but to keep going unless they wanted to die. I always wondered what they were thinking when the Red Sea parted, opening a passage towards freedom for them. I am sure some Israelites needed urging to move forward in their fear. God equipped them at the exact moment of the parting sea. Can you imagine if they had been given a day's notice of 'what was going to happen?' Don't you think most of the Israelites would have stayed behind, hoping they could survive the attack of the army who was after them? God did not give them time! They had to GO or DIE!

When I think back, I can remember so many times where God has equipped me for what I needed to do at just the right time. He equipped me to take care of my little boys alone after I left my first husband. He equipped me with a job making minimum wage, which was enough to support them. He equipped me to walk in faith when I was diagnosed with MS. He helped me to talk to the disease in a way that made me stronger and made me stubborn enough to NOT accept it. God equipped me with a new belief that I had not had before—when I was still taking shots to slow the progression of the disease—and it was enough for me to move forward with my head held high and with my story of how God heals. Did all the symptoms go away? No, but my fear went away because of the new belief God equipped me with in my spirit. I was able to confess my healing without resistance to others in my midst who did not understand because I *knew* what He had done for me and nothing else mattered.

God equipped me to go through the biggest heart break of my life when my Blake died in that plane crash. If I did not have God equipping me in these different events in my life, I know that my life now would look totally different. I think the point we need to remember about God equipping us is that He is always there to get us through whatever we are going through. He is always there in the good and bad times. He wants us to be aware of his presence in the *present*. He wants us to understand His faithfulness. Whatever you need, He will supply it. It is our choice to accept his guidance and the equipping He gives us.

If you are still doubting you are equipped to do something or questioning if God can really use you, remember this: Jacob cheated, Peter had a temper, David had an affair, Noah got drunk, Jonah ran from God, Moses committed murder, Gideon was insecure, Miriam gossiped, Martha worried, Thomas doubted, Sara was impatient, Elijah was moody, Zacchaeus was short, Abraham was old, and Lazarus was dead. God doesn't call the qualified; He qualifies the called. If you know you are not perfect but that God is still working on and using you, share this message.

CREATIVE

Creative: *Having the quality or power of creating; imaginative, expressive*

Gen 1:1 reads, "In the beginning God created the heavens and the earth." This is the first scripture of the Bible. God *created*. The fact that He created us in His image means that we have that same creativeness. God created Adam as a living being in His image. **Gen 1:26-27** reads, "He created light and darkness, he created everything we see today." **Gen 2:19** reads, "And out of the ground the Lord God formed every beast and living creature of the field and every bird of the air and brought them to Adam to see what he would call them and whatever Adam called every living creature, that was its name."

In her Study Bible, Joyce Meyer talks about how, not only is God creative in Genesis, but he asks Adam to be creative, too, by naming all the birds and animals. We need variety in our lives and sometimes that means that we need to change our creativity up. For many people, the thought of change is terrifying. Some people keep the same job or live in the same area all their lives because they feel those environments and activities are safe. People will stick to the familiar, whether they like where they are or not. Meyer states that, "God has created us to need diversity and variety. We are designed to require freshness and newness in our lives, and there is nothing wrong with feeling that you 'just need a change.' Stay within reason, but don't be afraid of the new. Embrace the fresh and different opportunities."

When I was sick in 2020 and I was doing dialysis from home for 14 hours a day, I knew I needed to do something intentional to keep my mind focused on God. One day, I was on social media, and I noticed a painting tutorial. I started watching it, and it was intriguing to me. I have never been an artist per se, but I loved the happy colors, and happy scenes in the painting. I paid a fee to participate in the tutorial and got some paints, and painting has become a new love for me. After the tutorial, I researched and found another mentor/teacher online and joined her classes and I was off to the races.

I loved painting. I painted angels, churches, flowers, barns, animals, mountains, all kinds of things. A friend of mine saw my paintings and she told me that I should sell them. For me, painting was never about the money, but if I could pay for my painting supplies, I would contribute 50% of my earnings to the local Kidney Foundation. The first time I posted about my work online, I sold 16 paintings. I was amazed at the response. This continued throughout the year. I gave some paintings to friends or people who might need a pick-me-up and I realized that I had more creativeness in me than I thought I did.

I encourage you to dig deep and find something that will bring you joy. It may not be painting. It may be gardening, or leading a Bible study group, or working with seniors, or volunteering in a nursing home. YOU ARE CREATIVE. GOD MADE YOU THAT WAY.

PURPOSE

Purpose: *An intended or desired result; the reason for which something exists or is done, made, used, etc.*

I love **Isaiah 61:1**. It reads, "The spirit of the Lord God is upon me, because the Lord has anointed and qualified me to preach the Gospel of good tidings to the meek, the poor, and afflicted; He has sent me to bind up and heal the brokenhearted, to proclaim liberty to the captives and the opening of the prison and of the eyes to those who are bound." There is more in verse 2, but if we just stop at verse 1, we learn that we are all here to declare God's message to those who don't know him. God has used my testimony to do that. He has used me to give other parents who have lost children new hope. He has used me to pray for and with my coworkers. If you have no idea what your purpose is, ask God about it. He will help you!

LOVED

Love: *A profound tender, passionate affection for another person.*

1 John 4: 15-19 reads, "If anyone acknowledges that Jesus is the Son of God, God lives in him and he in God. And so, we know and rely on the love God has for us. God is love. Whoever lives in love lives in God, and God in him ...There is no fear in love. But perfect love drives out fear because fear has to do with punishment. The one who fears is not made perfect in love."

I mentioned before that, when I went on a Walk to Emmaus, I learned how much God loved me. I learned that he wanted a relationship with me. I can still remember how I felt and how it changed my life. My love for God had reached a whole new level. I wanted to spend time with him, so I started journaling, I got involved in church groups. The more time I spent with Him, the more I wanted to be with Him.

In the Ukraine, I felt the strength of his love once again in the first church in which we taught. The church had a beautiful worship team and, the morning before I headed out to go to Ivano-Frankivsk to preach, I walked into the sanctuary to find the worship team singing the song that we played at Blake's Celebration Service, "I Can Only Imagine." They were singing in their language and it was beautiful. I will never forget how the presence of the Holy Spirit engulfed me as I sat in the pew and as they worshiped God with their voices. God was showing His love for me again.

CHOSEN

Chosen: (choose) to select from several possibilities, picked by preference. To want, desire.

Jeremiah 1:5 reads, "Before I formed you in the womb, I knew you: Before you were born, I sanctified you (chose you and set you apart). I ordained you a prophet to the nations" (Joyce Meyer, Study Bible). I love this verse. We all want other people to like us and approve of us, but we can only truly satisfy our desire for approval by receiving God's acceptance and approval. God told Jeremiah that, before He formed him in the womb of his mother, He knew and approved him as His chosen instrument. When God says He knows us, He means *He knows us*. It is a knowing that leaves nothing out. In **Jeremiah 1:8**, God tells Jeremiah not to be afraid of people's faces, because we tend to watch people's faces and see if they approve or disapprove of everything about us— what we are wearing, our hair, our performance. We pay too much attention to how people respond to us. God does not see our imperfections; he looks at our hearts and belief. In Jeremiah, He saw faith, and a deep desire to please God. And Jeremiah did answer to the call of God on his life. Despite criticism, un- popularity, and attacks against him, he faithfully delivered God's message as directed.

Being Chosen is one of the most exciting things about the Gospel to me. When God chooses us, He sanctifies us and sets us apart. When I got sick with kidney failure, last year, and found out that the odds of the disease I contracted were 1 in 1.6 million people to get it, I was amazed. And, of course as time went on, I accepted this and used it to give God glory. I praise God we are all chosen to be a part of His kingdom and messengers. Let God flow in you like a channel. You are special to God, and He has a special plan for you!

ACCEPTED

Accepted: approved, usually regarded as normal, right

As shown above in **Jeremiah 1:5**, God told Jeremiah that He knew him and approved of him before he was formed in his mother's womb. He said He KNEW Jeremiah, He was not speaking of a casual acquaintance, but of the deepest, most intimate knowledge. God may not always approve of the way we act, the way we sin, the ways we live our lives, however, he approves of us as his chosen instruments. Again, Joyce Meyer states that "if we live with feelings that God disapproves of us, we will always have the wrong kind of fear of Him, and that will hinder us from enjoying an intimate relationship with Him. Press forward in faith. Without faith, we can't please him. Whom do you want to please? I am sure it is God, so begin right now by living in the freedom of realizing that God knows you and approves of you as His chosen instrument" (Page 1146).

A part of your identity should be that you are ACCEPTED BY GOD. We are His. Even after my divorce, I felt guilty for taking my boys out of an environment of security, but I also knew God accepted me anyway. He was walking with me daily, even in my ignorance of how much He loved me.

HIS GRACE IS SUFFICIENT

Grace: favor or goodwill; elegance or beauty of form, manner, motion, or action.

1 Cor 12: 9 reads, "But He said to me, my grace is enough for you, for My strength and power are made perfect and show themselves most effective in weakness. Therefore, I will more gladly glory in my weaknesses and infirmities that the strength and power of Christ may rest upon me!" I have learned so much about God's grace. During my most difficult experiences, he was working with me 100% of the time, day and night. He was showing me His Grace. He always showed me a next step, even in the times that I was not praying. Through Blake's death—through all the emotions, through all the things that took place, through my numbness—His grace was sufficient. I encourage you to spend some time in reflection to see the times God has given you grace and helped you through situations you did not know you could get through. He has abundant love for you and has favor and goodwill for you. And it is in a form of beauty. Open your heart, receive it. Walk in it.

HIS ANGELS HAVE CHARGE OVER YOU

Angel: *one of a class of spiritual beings, a celestial attendant of God. A messenger, a person who performs a mission of God*

Psalm 91:11 reads, "He gives His angels charge over you to watch you in all your ways," and, as illustrated in my stories about Blake, this is such a special promise to me. God gave me a vision of a huge angel wing and I felt a rush of wind cross my face as I felt God whisper to me that He had Blake before he hit the ground. What a peace to carry with you, that His angels have charge over you. The entire passage of **Psalm 91** was so powerful during my 2020 health challenges, too. When I got home from the hospital, I wrote the entire chapter on large colored stock card and put them on my cabinets all around my kitchen so I would see them every day. I was still praying for a new kidney, I was sick from dialysis, and I felt bad daily, but seeing God's word and reading it out loud grounded me again so I could move forward. It is a phenomenal passage and promise that we are protected by His angels.

BLESSED COMING AND GOING

Blessed: *consecrated, sacred, hold, sanctified, divinely or supremely favored*

Deuteronomy 28:6 reads, "Blessed shall you be when you come in and blessed shall you be when you go out." This is such a special promise to me. I can relate it to my kidney transplant and many other events. The day we walked into that hospital for the kidney transplant, I had Scott, Tiffany, Chelsea, and Tommy with me. I felt so blessed to have my family there. I felt blessed coming in—making it through surgery with a new kidney and a good report—and blessed going out. God's word and promises are a foundation for the Christian life. When we can really grasp everything that God is doing in our lives (and what He has done in our lives) it can infinitely sustain our faith walk and our beliefs.

UNCOMMON WISDOM, UNCOMMON JOY, UNCOMMON PEACE

Uncommon: *Not common, unusual, rare, exceptional, remarkable.*

When I first read about this in this declaration statement, it became one of my favorite sections. As I think about having uncommon wisdom, joy, and peace, I want to go back to the Peace Plan from the previous chapter and tie these ideas together. You can only have that rare wisdom and joy and peace because you have the favor of God on your life, and because you have sought a strong relationship with Him by committing your ways to Him. You may have a yearning to spend time with Him often, and God also wants to spend time with you. He wants us to want Him. He wants us to seek him. He tells us this in **Luke 11: 9-13** and in **Matthew 7:7-11**. He encourages us to keep asking, seeking, and knocking, continually until it becomes a part of who we are.

So don't be afraid to ask. We have not because we ask not. When we seek, we will find Him. When we knock, the door will be opened. We must continue praising Him for what He is doing and He will continue to bless us with uncommon wisdom, joy, and peace. Not everyone seeks to find this. He knows our hearts and He wants to grant the desires of our hearts! Ask Him for the desires of your heart, then get ready for the ride of your life!

GOD IS YOUR VINDICATOR

Vindicator: someone that clears someone from blame or doubt

I love this statement in this declaration: God is my vindicator. He will fight for me! **Isaiah 54:17** reads, "No weapon forged against you will prevail, and you will refute every tongue that accuses you. This is the heritage of the servants of the Lord, and this is their vindication from me." This verse reminds me of when I was in the hospital again, and God said, "Quit fighting. I will fight for you." I knew the enemy was trying to take me out and I was trying to do all that I could to survive, but I was so tired. I knew I could not give up. I also knew I was fighting against a spiritual darkness that was not of God. In His faithfulness, though, God stepped in to protect me and I let Him fight. What a peace plan to *know* that no *weapon formed* against us will prosper as you serve God.

By breaking down this Declaration, I hope to help you to see that you have a God who loves you SO MUCH. You have a God who wants to encourage you because He has a destiny for your life. He wants you to know that you are equipped to do whatever you need to do, even if you doubt it now. He wants you to know that you are creative, as you were created in His image. You are loved, chosen, and ACCEPTED by this almighty God. There is NOTHING you can do to make Him love you more, and there is nothing you can do to make Him love you less. I think people can get confused by this. They don't understand the gift that God has given them. At the cross, it is finished! When you decide to follow Christ, it is finished. Your sins are forgiven, and your slate is clean. It is finished. You don't have to perform acts, go to church every Sunday, pray all the time, or perform for God. He loves you—period. And, if you sin tomorrow, it does not change His mind about you. His grace is sufficient for you and

His angels have charge over you. You truly are blessed coming in and going out. It is a promise in His Word.

I pray you can reach a point that you have uncommon wisdom, uncommon joy, and uncommon peace. It is a process. It takes time in the presence of the Lord and in His word, but if that is something you truly want, I would ask Him to show you what that looks like for you. Because of the difficult experiences I have gone through, the words God has spoken to me, and the lessons He has taught me, I am uncommonly wise, joyful, and peaceful. This is not a boast; it is a place of peace in my heart that I can always call on when I need Him. Because God is my VINDICATOR, and He is *your* vindicator, and He fights for you! You just get to choose to believe that and walk in His truth.

From all the stories I have shared, I can sum up the things I want you to take away. If you have ever felt like a failure, had a fear of the unknown, had a broken heart, didn't know your path in this world, been confused because you thought things were settled and the enemy came back to fight you again...I pray this book touched you and you can walk away with some clarity on your experiences. May you be encouraged with the message about G.R.A.C.E, to be obedient and just GO in order to watch the blessings flow. May you use this declaration to remember who you are, how God feels about you, and how He protects and equips you for your purpose! And, most importantly, may you remember my message of

HOPE because you are still breathing, and you must keep moving and let God fight for you. There is always hope. Keep this statement in your memory bank so you can recall it when you need it:

"Even in the worst time of life, if you are still breathing, that means you are still alive. If you are still here, you haven't accomplished what is still to be accomplished. The most important part of your life is still ahead of you."
—Andy Andrews

References

Meyer, Joyce. "Life Points ." *The Everyday Life Bible* , First ed., Warner Faith Hachett Book Group, New York, NY, 2006.

The NIV Study Bible, Zondervan, GRAND RAPIDS, MI, 1995. Copyright 1985, 1995, 2002 by Zondervan. All rights reserved.

Peterson, Eugene H. *Message Remix: Bonded 2.0,* The Message, 2006. Scripture taken from the message—Copyright 1993, 1994, 1995, 1996, 2000, 2001, 2002. Used by permission of NavPress Publishing Group

The Passion Translation, *New Testament with Psalms, Proverbs, and Song of Songs, Second Edition Copyright 2018 Passion & Fire Ministries*

YouVersion Bible App online, version 9.31, RED 3.7.0.5158

Dictionary.com mobile app. Version 9.11.1.2 2018

Publisher is not responsible for validity of information taken from online apps.

About the Author

Nancy Ormon has a purpose to give others hope and to teach of God's amazing love. She is an author, artist, speaker and loves the ministry. She is a mother of 3, a Nana to two beautiful granddaughters and a good friend to many. She is gifted with compassion and encouragement. She loves journaling, painting, playing golf and spending time with her family. She and her husband of 39 years, Tommy, make their home in Lubbock, Texas.

CONTACT INFORMATION

Email: Nancy.ormon@yahoo.com
Website: https://nancyormon.com/

Can You Help?

Bumblebee from Ukraine

Thank You For Reading My Book!

I really appreciate all of your feedback, and I love hearing what you have to say.

I need your input to make the next version of this book and my future books better.

Please leave me an honest review on Amazon letting me know what you thought of the book.

If you know me personally, please just talk about the book in the review, and not focus how we know each other.

Thanks so much!
Nancy Ormon

Made in the USA
Coppell, TX
07 April 2022

76196953R00083